Christine Bille Nielsen & Tina Scheftelowitz

VEGETARIAN
WITH A
VENGEANCE

GRUB STREET | LONDON

ABOUT THE RECIPES

>> All the recipes are for four people, unless otherwise indicated.

>> All fresh ingredients are given in unprepared quantities unless otherwise indicated.

>> In some of the recipes we have used vegetable stock. The simplest way to use this is by adding water and vegetable stock separately directly into the dish. It is not necessary to dissolve the vegetable stock in boiling water before adding it to the dish. Read more about good quality vegetable stock on page 216.

>> The oven temperature given is without fan, unless otherwise indicated. If you use a fan oven the temperature should be approx. 10% or approx. 20 degrees lower. You should use the fan oven if you have several dishes in the oven at the same time, or if you want a particularly crisp finish. Otherwise the fan oven will use more electricity, damaging the environment and may also dry out the food.

>> Read about special products and find out where to buy them on pages 216-217.

>> Read tips about beans, vegetables and kitchen utensils on pages 221, 222 and 225.

>> Mix and match the recipes from different sections and you will have a complete meal. Read more on page 10.

Symbols used in the book

>> Vegan dishes are marked with

>> Honey may be substituted with other sweetener or another ingredient may be left out/substituted. And then the dish is vegan

>> The dish is suitable for packed lunches

contents

FULL BLOODED
or PART TIME VEGETARIAN?

You can be a 'plant eater' in many different ways. Maybe you are 100% vegetarian with several years of being vegetarian behind you. Maybe you are the gastronomic head of a family who have discovered the pleasures of several meat free days, either for the sake of the environment or for ethical reasons by not eating animals. Maybe you are contemplating becoming vegetarian for health reasons. Or maybe you like vegetables so much that you want less meat on your plate everyday.

No matter what type of vegetarian you are, or think of becoming, this book is sliced, boiled, fried and baked for you and your fellow diners. For your inspiration and for whetting your appetite. For putting an end to myths and prejudices. And for furthering the good, green taste.

With this book you will enjoy preparing vegetarian food every day which is filling from morning to night. You will get ideas for combining the dishes for green colourful party food. And of course we have made room for the sweet finale, the packed lunches and the good bread.

Taste of vegetables
The book is written by two cooks and luckily we experience taste differently. Bille loves mild, delicate flavours and lots of fresh herbs. Tina wants to use all the spices.

We love each other's food, so instead of agreeing about pinches of this and that, we have let the individual rule in the different recipes. That is why the dishes predominantly have either one or the other character serving the common language of good flavour.

The food must taste to make the angels sing in order to make it through our gastronomic sieve and onwards into the book.

Eat with laughter and joy
There are hundreds of health warnings which

one could easily incorporate into a vegetarian cookbook. Instead of backing certain healthy hobby horses, we have decided that primarily our green food should taste good. That is why, for example, we have not used meat substitute products such as quorn and 'soy meat'. It simply does not taste good enough for us to want to spend energy on it.

The good news for bean fiends and vegetable guys
It is a mistake to believe that healthy food is ascetic and unsexy and that delicious tasting food and health are incompatible. We aim to make food where the two are not in each others' way but meet in a loving embrace.

The key word is balance between the salty, the acidic, the sweet and the bitter, supplemented with plenty of herbs and spices and a little fat for flavour – then the food will automatically taste good. You do not need oceans of cream, butter or cheese in order to get the desired effect. But sometimes you need it in small doses, because the dish demands it.

We are also a pair of stubborn wholemeal women with a mission. That is why we are using wholemeal varieties of grain, pasta, buckwheat, noodles, rice etc. They not only taste good but are also much healthier than their refined counterparts. For the same reason we have used lots of coarse vegetables such as cabbage and root vegetables in the service of the green message.

Finally we have avoided any type of light product. We would rather have a small amount of good, full fat cheese than a large piece of a low fat poor tasting one. See also the section about the healthiest oils on page 218.

For city- and suburban vegetarians
You don't need to have a bio dynamic herb

bed in the back garden to join the green wave with this book in your hand. It has been written for anyone who lives in the city, the suburbs or the provinces without access to cultivated earth.

The book's recipes have all been prepared with ingredients available from the nearest supermarket supplemented with specialities from ethnic stores and health food shops. Cress on the window sill is therefore enough in order to get on with this book.

Saving the world in a fruit loving fashion

Admittedly we are not ourselves full-time vegetarians. But we love fruit and vegetables and could easily live on them by themselves, if we had to.

And then we like many of the thoughts which make more and more people choose a green life style – whether they go all the way or only part of the way. It is scientifically and passionately proven that green food is the most sustainable choice we as consumers can make compared to all the other choices we are faced with. Whether it is climate, resources, the welfare of animals, the distribution of food worldwide, ecology, health or private finances, the green menu has an enormous head start.

So if you want to make a difference you can take a big step just by eating a little more green than you did before. For example, just by starting little by little and introducing a vegetarian day or two a week at home or by letting the green play the main role in the meal.

It is our hope that this cookbook will give a lot of good people the desire and pleasure for more vegetarian habits – maybe even deliver growth for a tiny beetroot revolution all around the world.

May the book inspire you to find your green point.

Regards
Christine Bille Nielsen and Tina Scheftelowitz

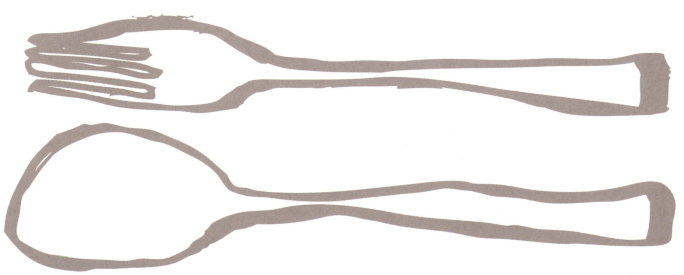

WISE – about being vegetarian

As we wrote in the introduction, this book is both for full time vegetarians – or for those planning to become full time vegetarians – and for those of you who want to turn up the green fire at home in the kitchen with meat free days or generally more greens on the plate.

If you leave meat out of your diet completely there are a few points you need to be aware of. Here follows a little background information about living as a vegetarian, good arguments for joining the green wave and a few practical hints on how to put your meals together, to make sure you and your family have all your requirements for vitamins, minerals, fibre etc covered.

Meat free or rich in plants?

You could choose to consider vegetarian food as a diet of exclusion, i.e. food where something is 'missing' – in this case animal produce. WE believe that is sad and the wrong way of embracing all the wonderful, green food and ingredients. Vegetarian food has in our view its own right. It is an accomplished whole which is not defined by being meat free but rather 'rich in plants'.

Vegetarian food is a horn of plenty of nature's wealth which pours forth out of the ground in front of our eyes in an explosion of colours, juice and power.

Vege Vikings

Serve vegetarian food to a Viking, and she will ask when the meat arrives. Place a classic meat dish in front of a Hindu who has never seen anything other that vegetarian food, and he will wonder when the food arrives since the steak or the chop takes up half the plate and gravy and potatoes the remainder.

Food is habit and habits are culture. It is therefore not so strange that vegetarianism causes astonishment in the western world. Vegetarianism is quite simply a completely different way of thinking about the food that most of us grew up with.

Meat with garnish

Traditionally, western food consists of variations on the theme of 'meat with garnish' – for example burgers or steaks with …. Vegetarian food turns this plate model upside down. A vegetarian meal is more like an equation where the order of the factors is immaterial. On a Wednesday evening in November at home with the family dinner might be a substantial salad, plus a ragout, plus a little bread plus something stir fried plus a small bowl of vegetable stick and dips.

Vegetarian variants

Vegetarians exist in many interesting versions. Some eat no meat or fish. End of story. Others also drop milk and butter. Some avoid eggs and honey since animals are part of the production. Others take a step further and would never dream of buying down duvets, leather jackets and woollen socks for the same reason. And the entirely fundamentalist live exclusively on fruit and berries which have fallen to the ground by themselves.

Between these extremes there are several curious variants. This is the entire spectrum and the possibilities:

Vegetarians

Lacto-ovo vegetarian: supplements plant food with eggs (ovo) and dairy products (lacto). Slang: Egg-tarian:

Vegans: avoid all animal produce, i.e. also eggs, dairy products and honey.

Raw food vegans: only eat raw vegetable foods or heated to max. 45 degrees C. In the UK and the USA 'raw food' has become very popular.

Sexual vegans: will only eat vegan food and does not have sex with meat eaters.

Fruitarian: only eat fruit, nuts, seeds, berries and other crops which can be picked without ruining the plant – the sub group 'fallen fruitarians' will only eat fallen fruit.

Semi-vegetarians

Some people mainly eat vegetarian food, but will now and then add fish or chicken. But even if it is the first step on the way to becoming a vegetarian, you are not a genuine vegetarian but in reality a sub group of meat eaters. Absorbing this information we now look at this sub group's variants:

Pescotarian: supplements plant food with fish, eggs and dairy products.

Pollotarian: supplements plant food with chicken, eggs and dairy products.

Flexitarian: is vegetarian most of the time but will eat meat now and then. Many people are probably flexitarians without knowing it themselves: All of us who place vegetables and fruit at the centre of the meal, and eat meat only when we go out for dinner or feel like a large, juicy steak. To be flexitarian is the easiest, most flexible way of getting more vegetables and less meat.

Frugarian: avoids buying products at all in protest against over production, the capitalist exploitation of people, animals and nature. Finds food in the open and in containers etc, but does not necessarily avoid animal produce.

Automatically healthier?

Vegetarian food is healthier for two reasons: You avoid the pitfalls of a meat dominated diet, i.e. too much saturated fat, too much protein and too little fibre. And you will benefit more through plant based food i.e. more fibre, useful micronutrients and a moderate amount of protein.

Remember though, that vegetarian food is not automatically healthier than a meat based diet. You will still have too much fat and sugar and too little fibre if you too often have pizza, omelette, cheese sandwiches and cakes! You need lots of vegetables, grain and legumes – both fresh and cooked – and plenty of variation during the week and month in order to harvest the full fruit of your vegetarian habits.

A more varied diet

Green food is an inspiration for a more varied diet since there are many different vegetarian raw ingredients compared to variants of meat and cuts – and thereby also more variety. So when the meat moves out, a lot of new possibilities move in.

However, it means that you should be inspired by the many possibilities and make sure that the food becomes varied and balanced with many different types of vegetables and a suitable amount of protein and good carbohydrates rich in fibre. And like everyone else – including meat eaters – not too much sugar or fat.

Important reasons for becoming vegetarian

Vegetarians can usually remember what made them become vegetarian and the reason for their decision to leave meat out. Later on they might find even more reasons which confirmed their choice. What was – or is – your reason for eating more vegetables?

Vegetarians:

>> live longer
>> have fewer cardio vascular diseases
>> have fewer risks of contracting a number of cancers
>> avoid entirely meat borne diseases such as salmonella and campylobacter
>> don't have to take medicine – and hormone residue from animal farming
>> receive fewer heavy metals and other harmful materials via the food since plant food is at the bottom of the food chain and therefore has accumulated the least in comparison with meat which is at the top of the food chain and therefore has accumulated the most toxic materials
>> will more easily get lots of fibre, the recommended 5 fruit and vegetables a day, antioxidants etc.
>> have less saturated fat
>> save on the food budget since green is generally cheaper than meat.

Source: (The Danish National Board of Health, WWF, British Medical Journal et al.

Green is of benefit in every way

IIf everyone in the UK had a meat free day a week, it would be the equivalent of taking 5 million cars off the road. See also http://www.animalaid.org.uk

However, the CO_2 accounts for vegetables also depend on whether they are grown in the open ground or under cover, how far they have been transported and whether it is by air, ship or lorry. For the environmental advantage to be complete it is preferable that the vegetables have been grown in the open ground and not transported too far.

A plus for the environment

Production of grain, fruit and vegetables:

>> emits less CO_2 (a steak 'costs' in CO_2 66 times as much as a portion of potatoes: A vegetarian saves the environment a total of approx 1 ton of CO_2 per annum)

>> uses up to 1000 times less water than meat production

>> uses less energy (for heating stables and for transport of fodder)

>> protects against over grazing, erosion and deforestation (e.g. 40% of the rain forest in South America has been cut down to make way for cattle production)

>> pollutes less (UK produces e.g. 9 million pigs a year, who produce tons of manure)

A plus for the world's food resources

It is a much better use of water, energy and nutrition to eat the crops directly from the soil instead of letting them pass through animals first and then eat the animal. The 'waste' of good proteins may be up to 90% by choosing the steak instead of the bean burger.

Converted to full stomachs, it means that the same amount of crops which are needed to produce half a kilo of meat may fill a meat eater, but approx. 25 vegetarians. On a global scale this means that we could feed the entire world's population every day, if we all were mainly vegetarians. Source WWF et al.

A plus for the animals

In conventional agriculture efficiency is so high that it harms the welfare of the animals – both before and on the way to the slaughterhouse. Not even modern fishing production with over fishing, discarded by-catch, large lake- and ocean- farms and medication is without problems for the fish and our conscience. If however, you choose free range meat, milk and eggs and/or organic farm produce, the animals will have had better conditions. But if you want to avoid the animal dilemmas entirely, the meat free life is the only way forward.

Enough food in the world......

The production of meat takes up a lot of room in the landscape. Agriculture produces and slaughters millions of animals every year – from pigs and chickens to ostriches and cows. These animals that are all plant eaters eat vast quantities of greens and grain every year – so much that we have to import several million tons a year.

If instead the raw materials were used for human consumption, The Compassion in World Farming Report 'Global Warning' states; A farmer can feed up to 30 persons throughout the year on one hectare with vegetables, fruits, cereals and vegetable fats. If the same area is used for the production of eggs, milk/meat the number of people fed varies from 5-10 (around 3 times less). Globally, a typical diet requires up to 5 times the amount of land compared to a vegan diet and 2.5 times the amount compared to a veggie diet.

Cold turkey or smooth transition

If you consider becoming 100% vegetarian there are two ways you can go about it in order to live a meat free life: 1) Cold turkey where you throw meat and fish overboard once and for all – or 2) the smooth transition where you leave meat out little by little and finally drop it entirely.

The vegetarian cold turkey

This demands that you a) first read about what you need in order to be 100% vegetarian, e.g. vegetables, legumes, grain and dairy products and b) give everything that has meat and animal products to a meat lover and equip your kitchen with the basic ingredients which will make life as a vegetarian a little easier and better tasting. See page 214.

The smooth transition to green

Start by 'turning the meal upside down' by letting the vegetables fill the bigger part of the meal and have meat as garnish. You could also choose food where the meat can easily be camouflaged, e.g. stews. In this way it is easy eventually to remove the meat entirely or replace it with non-animal 'filling' e.g. beans and lentils

Variation over time

Not only vegetarians, but everyone including children and adults should eat a varied diet. What does a varied diet mean and how do I do it? As a main rule choose
>> to combine the various foodstuffs e.g. vegetables, legumes and grain in a balanced way, i.e. do not eat too little or too much from each group.
>> between the individual foodstuffs in a group, so you don't only eat e.g. sliced cheese from ' the dairy group' but also milk, cottage cheese, yogurt etc.
>> vary food over time i.e. for meals during the day, week and the month.

This book is easy to use for varying your diet, since it is divided into chapters where you can pick and choose from a cross section of all the recipes. Combine a meal with dishes from several different chapters. And make it different from day to day and week to week. In a month you will have eaten your way through lots of vegetarian variation and flavours without thinking about it. We have also varied the recipes themselves so they often contain several types of vegetables with different characteristics.

How many meals per day?

As a vegetarian you can easily maintain the principle of three main meals a day supplemented with two-three good snacks.

Vegetarian food can fill you for just as long as a meat based diet, but there may be a tendency for the lighter vegetarian dishes to make your stomach clock ring a little more often, since vegetables for a large part consist of water which does not fill you for quite as long.

If you eat a lot of salads and green dishes without much rice, pasta, bread or beans, you maybe need a few more filling snacks with extra bread and fruit and greens.

Am I getting enough?

Are you getting enough iron as a vegetarian? How about proteins? And was there not something about a vitamin which you can only get from meat? These are the most commonly asked questions — and the wonderfully simple answer is:

Protein

Is found in both animal and vegetable foods. Plant food is rich in protein, in particular beans, nuts, seeds, quinoa, bread, grain, lentils, rice and pasta. It is a common misunderstanding that vegetarians do not get enough protein. If you eat a varied vegetarian diet, you will automatically cover your needs — especially if you also eat eggs, cheese and milk products.

Iron

Is found in all types of foodstuffs. There might be a lot of iron in vegetarian food, but it is a type which the body has more difficulty in absorbing compared to the iron found in meat. Broccoli, spinach, green cabbage, lentils and beans are some of the many plant foods, which contain plenty of iron. The body can most easily absorb iron if you eat it with food rich in vitamin C. And at the same time avoid food with a large calcium content, e.g. milk products, since calcium inhibits the uptake of iron.

Vitamin B 12

Is found in meat, milk products and eggs. Therefore it is recommended that vegans, to be on the safe side, but not vegetarians, take a Vitamin B 12 supplement in the form of a daily vitamin pill.

Calcium

Is found in milk, cheese, eggs, green vegetables and fish. Both vegetarians and vegans get sufficient amounts provided they regularly eat foods rich in calcium such as dried beans, seeds, nuts, seaweed and green leaf vegetables.

The family's small green-eaters

You can easily let your children eat vegetarian food as their first solids. For children as for adults the same rules apply for having a varied diet in the meal itself and during the day and during the month.

Young children have small stomachs and therefore do not eat large quantities at one time. Since vegetarian food generally 'fills' more of the plate, in order to fill you up for a long time, you must make sure that there is sufficient energy in the food your child is eating, in particular in the form of fat. http://www.vegsoc.org/info/

Among cookbooks you could also look at *Vegetarian Food for Children* by Nicola Graimes.

How to wean children to vegetarian food

It is of course easier, if the children are used to eating vegetarian food from a young age. Older children can learn to eat vegetarian food and more greens by starting with familiar dishes that they like, e.g. falafel, sushi, pies, burgers, filled pancakes, pizza, spring rolls, wraps, hummus, pasta with sauces, lasagne, creamy potatoes and noodle soup. See the recipes in this book.

Pregnant and vegetarian

You are vegetarian and now pregnant, what do you do? As you have always done, eat healthily and varied, follow the general advice on diet for pregnant women and avoid meat and fish. The Vegetarian Society has an excellent booklet on pregnancy and babies http://www.vegsoc.org/info/preg.html. They say; women trying to conceive are advised to take a 400 microgram supplement (400µg) of folic acid every day, from the time you stop using contraception to the twelfth week of your pregnancy. The rest will follow. After delivery you follow the general advice about diet for new mothers. If you are breast feeding it is particularly important that you take plenty of fluid and rest well during the day.

It takes time for the body to recover after a birth and to get back to normal, and you will be helping it well on the way with a healthy and nutritious diet. Food after birth is the best gift you can receive – and give.
Tell family and friends that you want homemade bread and plenty of wonderful, vegetarian dishes for the table and for the freezer. Maybe they will be inspired by the recipes in this book.

Hidden animal produce

Many prepared food products have hidden animal ingredients: It may be pig fat in biscuits and cakes and gelatin (based on animal protein) in sweets, desserts and ice cream. Intestinal enzymes are used for the production of cheese, and insects called cochineal for adding colour to sweet drinks and Campari.

How do vegetarians avoid these hidden animal ingredients? The easiest way is to buy your ingredients processed as little as possible – i.e. taken directly out of the soil or picked from plants.

Mix and match your food

Vegetarian food breaks with many meat-tied conventions. Therefore this book has not been arranged in the traditional way with first courses, main dishes, desserts etc. The chapters are designed so you can pick from them across the book and in this way easily put a healthy meal together according to your own taste.

The chapters have been arranged according to the consistency, texture and taste experience which the dishes will give you. For example the chapter 'firm' is the vegetarian's answer to meat and fish. Hot & filling is pasta, potatoes, rice and grain, while sliced is a chapter with salads. The idea is that you mix a meal by matching dishes from the different chapters. In this way you will feel full and have a wonderful experience of taste. Take for example a quinoa bun from the chapter 'firm' combined with a bean salad from the chapter 'sliced' and a mushroom sauce from the chapter 'saucy'.

This is how you mix and match yourself

To mix means taking dishes from various chapters so you have several different textures and tastes on your plate. By mixing dishes, you will cover your nutritional needs, taste and texture (creamy, finely sliced, chopped, baked, substantial light, etc).

To match means choosing dishes from all the chapters which you think will taste good together. Maybe they come from the same region, e.g. an Indian dahl from the pot with a raita from sliced and a pilau from hot & filling. If you like to combine dishes differently do just that. You can also mix the dishes in this book with your own favourite dishes and favourite recipes from other books.

This is how the book helps you to mix and match

If you believe it is a little complicated to mix and match on your own you can take the quick shortcut: Leaf through the book and choose a dish which you think looks delicious. For each dish we have recommended what goes with it.

small dishes
first courses
snacks
quick bites

This chapter contains some delicious first courses or dishes which you can serve when you are not particularly hungry. You can also prepare several small dishes and serve them as tapas.

Quails eggs and greens with dukkah

Ingredients

½ - 1 fennel or vegetables of
  your choice
16 small boiled potatoes
8 boiled quails eggs
Toothpicks
Good quality olive oil

Dukkah

30 g hazelnuts
2 tsp whole coriander
1½ tsp cumin seeds
2 tbsp sesame seeds
1 large pinch cayenne pepper/
  freshly ground black pepper
½ tsp salt

>> Chop the nuts medium coarse, use a food processor, if necessary.

>> Grind coriander and cumin coarsely with a mortar and pestle or coffee grinder. You can also use a mini chopper for both spices, but chop the nuts and spices separately. Mix the nuts and the spices with sesame seeds, cayenne pepper or pepper and salt.

>> Toast the mixture at high heat in a frying pan and turn all the time until golden and fragrant. Remove from the pan immediately.

>> Or toast in a thin layer in a dish in the oven at 180C/gas 4 for 10-15 minutes. Stir a few times during cooking.

>> Serve sliced fennel, boiled potatoes and unpeeled boiled quails eggs in a dish, serve a bowl with dukkah and one with olive oil and leave the guests to dip the items first in the olive oil and then in the dukkah.

! Remove the small bits from the chopped nuts prior to roasting to avoid them burning. Crumble the nuts between your fingers over the frying pan/oven dish. This will separate the small bits and leave them behind on the chopping board and you can add them after/at the last minute for roasting.

! You can use all kinds of vegetables and serve them with good bread which is broken into smaller pieces.

Potatoes

Fennel

Quails eggs

Olive oil

Dukkah

Avocado with SUSHI-GINGER and sesame

This is a quick first course where you serve avocadoes cut in half, then sprinkled with lemon- or lime juice, filled with sushi-ginger and sprinkled with toasted sesame seeds. Serve with salt or soy sauce.

Bombay Bloody Mary SHOT

50 g celery with top removed
500 ml tomato juice
½ clove garlic, finely chopped
Cayenne pepper, to taste
Salt
1 tbsp vodka (optional)

Topping
100 g Greek yogurt 10% fat
¾ tsp curry powder
¼ tsp ground cumin
¼ tsp honey
Salt

Garnish
Celery
Curry powder

>> Slice the celery as finely as possible. Mix with tomato juice, chopped garlic, cayenne pepper and salt and season to taste.

>> Mix yogurt, curry powder, cumin, honey and salt and adjust to taste. Place in the refrigerator until ready to serve.

>> Cut 4 small celery mixing- sticks with the top left on.

>> To serve: If you like, add 1 tbsp vodka to each glass, and pour the tomato juice into the glasses. Top up with yogurt, sprinkle with curry powder and place a 'mixing stick' in each glass.

! Buy a top quality tomato juice. Available from health food shops or good supermarkets.

! Instead of quinoa you could use brown jasmine- or basmati rice. Cook as indicated on the packet. Read about quinoa and seaweed on pages 216-217.

Cones of seaweed with QUINOA and avocado cream

Makes 12

100 ml whole quinoa (approx.
  300 ml boiled)
175 ml water
½ yellow or red sweet pepper
6 sheets nori
1 small bunch of fresh
  coriander

Avocado cream

2 ripe avocadoes
1 clove garlic
1 lime
salt

≫ Place the quinoa in a sieve and rinse in cold water. Boil in a saucepan under a lid in 175 ml water for 10 minutes, remove from the heat, add salt and set aside with the lid on top for 10 minutes. All the water should now be absorbed. If not, pour into a sieve and drain or leave for a little while longer. Leave the quinoa to cool.

≫ Remove the seeds from the sweet pepper and slice finely.

≫ Cut the seaweed sheets across lengthwise.

≫ Cream: Blend the avocado flesh with garlic and add lime juice and salt to taste. Or press the garlic and mash it all together with a fork.

≫ To serve: Place the seaweed, the quinoa, fresh coriander and the sweet pepper in a serving dish and the avocado cream in a bowl, so each person can roll the cones themselves.

≫ Take a piece of seaweed. Add 1-2 tbsp of quinoa to one half, a few slices of sweet pepper, some coriander and 1-2 tsp avocado cream on top. Roll the seaweed round the filling like a cone. Eat immediately while the seaweed is still crisp.

Vegetables baked with
MANGO-SOY MARINADE

Use the vegetables in season, see the seasonal chart page 226

**16 slices/pieces of
vegetables of your choice,
e.g. squash, mushrooms
without stalks, aubergine,
parsnip, Hamburg parsley,
celeriac.**

**1 lime, cut into quarters for
serving**

Marinade

1 ripe mango
2-3 tbsp soy sauce
Approx. 2 tsp clear honey
**1 clove garlic, peeled and cru-
shed**
Cayenne pepper to taste

➤➤ Slice the vegetables into ½ cm thick slices and place on a baking tray lined with baking paper.

➤➤ Slice the flesh of the mango. Blend with soy sauce, honey, garlic and cayenne pepper to a uniform puree and season to taste. Set half of the puree aside for later.

➤➤ Pour the rest of the marinade over the vegetables.

➤➤ Bake the vegetables in the oven at 200C/gas 6 shortly before serving for approx. 15 minutes.

➤➤ Arrange the rest of the marinade over the vegetables and serve with the lime quarters for drizzling on top of the vegetables.

Vegelex
The word vegetarian
(people who live on
fruit and vegetables)
was invented by the
world's first vegeta-
rian association,
The British Vege-
tarian Society 150
years ago. The word
derives from the
Latin *vegetus* which
means 'alive, full of
life, fresh and he-
althy' and has nothing
directly to do with
the word to vegetate.

TOFU with topping

Read about tofu and miso on page 216.

300 g firm tofu, silken style

Miso sauce

2 tbsp miso, red if available
½ clove garlic, finely chopped
1 tsp dark sesame oil
1 tbsp lime juice
1 tbsp water
1 tbsp maple syrup

Topping

1 red apple or 1 pear
Lime juice
Watercress, cress, bean sprouts
  or pea sprouts
Chilli flakes (optional)

>> Mix the miso with the garlic, sesame oil, lime juice, water and maple syrup and season to taste.

>> Cut the tofu carton open and let the tofu slide carefully out onto a chopping board. Leave it to drain on a tea towel or a piece of kitchen towel.

>> Cut the tofu into cubes of approx. 2 x 2 cm and arrange on plates or on a serving dish.

>> Cut the apple into small cubes of approx. ½ x ½ cm and mix with the lime juice.

>> To serve: Arrange the miso sauce over the tofu and sprinkle with apple, the greens and chilli flakes, if you wish.

Vegetable sticks with MISO DIP

Choose one or the other dip or serve half a portion of each. Use seasonal vegetables, see the seasonal chart, page 226.

500 g vegetables, e.g. radish, celery, carrot, sweet pepper, cucumber, cauliflower or Chinese radish.

Bille's miso dip
4 tbsp miso, red if available
½ clove garlic, finely chopped
1 tsp honey
1 tsp dark sesame oil
5 tbsp water

Tina's miso dip
4 tbsp miso, red if available
2½ tbsp honey or maple syrup
2 tbsp cider vinegar or other vinegar
A little water, if necessary

>> Cut the carrot, cucumber, sweet pepper, celery and Chinese radish into small sticks. Cut the cauliflower into small florets and leave ordinary radishes whole.

>> Mix the ingredients for the chosen dip and stir until smooth. Season to taste.

>> Serve the vegetables with miso dip in a bowl for dipping.

For texture the dishes in this chapter contain the firm ingredient. They are either complete suggestions in themselves or items which you can combine with sauces, salads or hot dishes.

Quinoa patties with BEETROOT

These are fabulous and bound to become winners! They taste delicious with an acidic garnish, e.g. the raw salad on page 84, one of the seasonal salads page 101 or a tzatziki page 98.

Makes 14

100 ml whole quinoa (300 ml boiled)
175 ml water
150 g beetroot
100 g onion
1 clove garlic, pressed through garlic press
100 ml coarse wholemeal flour (or coarse spelt flour)
2 tsp curry powder
1 tsp salt
2 eggs
Neutral tasting oil (such as rapeseed oil) or olive oil for frying

➤➤ Rinse the quinoa in a sieve in cold water. Boil in 175 ml water for 10 minutes under a lid. Remove the saucepan from the heat, mix in a little salt and leave on one side for 10 minutes under a lid.

➤➤ Peel the beetroot, peel the onion and grate both coarsely on a grater.

➤➤ Put garlic, wholemeal – or spelt – flour, curry powder and salt in a bowl together with the grated vegetables. Mix in the boiled quinoa and then the eggs. If the quinoa has cooled just add everything to the bowl at the same time. Leave the mixture to rest for a little while you prepare the garnish.

➤➤ Place 1 heaped tbsp of the mixture per pattie in a hot frying pan with oil and press them out to approx. 1½ cm high. Turn down the heat to medium and continue frying for approx. 5 minutes on each side until firm, brown and crisp.

Firm

! You could use rice or brown rice, bulgur or couscous instead of quinoa. Any root vegetable could be used instead of beetroot.

! Add 50 g feta cut into cubes and then leave out ½ tsp salt or add 50 g grated cheese of your choice.

! Make the patties in advance and heat in the oven at 200C/gas 6 for approx. 15 minutes.

! The patties are also delicious as burgers. In this case make them twice as big. The mixture makes 6-7 burgers. See suggestions for burger page 178.

Spinach quenelles with TOMATO sauce

Serve these spinach quenelles with good bread and a bowl of crisp salad. Remember to defrost the spinach, overnight in the fridge.

Tomato sauce

100 g onion
2 cloves garlic, chopped
1 tbsp olive oil
400 g tin peeled tomatoes
1 tsp salt
Freshly ground pepper
1 handful coarsely chopped
   fresh basil

Spinach quenelles

500 g frozen chopped spinach
2 eggs
8 tbsp (70 g) plain white flour
1 tsp salt
Freshly ground pepper
250 g ricotta
50 g freshly grated parmesan
1 pinch ground nutmeg

To sprinkle on top

50 g freshly grated parmesan

>> The tomato sauce: Peel the onion and chop it. Lightly fry the onion and garlic in the oil in a saucepan for 1 minute.

>> Blend the tomatoes and mix with the onions. Let the sauce boil under a lid for 15 minutes. Meanwhile prepare the spinach quenelles. Add salt and pepper to taste, and mix in the basil just before serving.

>> Spinach quenelles: Squeeze the water out of the spinach without drying it out completely.

>> Mix the spinach thoroughly with eggs, plain flour, salt, pepper, ricotta, parmesan and nutmeg.

>> Bring 3 litres of lightly salted water to the boil in a saucepan. Turn down the heat to simmering point. Using two dessert spoons shape the spinach into quenelles the size of small eggs and place them carefully in the boiling water. Dip the spoon in the water between forming each quenelle. Leave the quenelles to simmer in the water until they all float to the surface.

>> Place the hot tomato sauce in a serving dish. Remove the spinach quenelles from the water, drain a little on a piece of kitchen towel. Place on top of the sauce. Sprinkle with parmesan and serve immediately.

! Ricotta is an Italian fresh cheese with not much taste but excellent texture. It is available from most supermarkets. You can use cottage cheese instead.

! If you want a slightly chunkier texture and can't be bothered to blend then use chopped tomatoes for the sauce.

Firm

Falafel
- fried spiced chickpea patties

A good falafel is crisp on the outside and soft, but cooked through on the inside. Serve with a crisp salad and tahini dressing (page 84) or 'the wild ' aubergine salad (page 94) in pita bread for example.

Makes 20

150 g dried chickpeas
2 handfuls fresh coriander or
   parsley
1 small (50 g) onion
2 cloves garlic
1½ tsp ground cumin
1½ tsp ground coriander
¼ tsp cayenne pepper
½ tsp salt
¼ tsp baking powder
2 tbsp plain white flour
750 ml neutral tasting rapeseed
   oil for cooking

Serve with
Sambal oelek or other chilli
   sauce

›› Soak the chickpeas in a large bowl of cold water for a minimum of 10 hours, overnight, if possible, in the fridge.

›› Pour away the water from the chickpeas and blend in a food processor with the coriander, the onion cut into quarters, garlic, spices, salt, baking powder and flour until you have a smooth dough.

›› Shape the falafel mixture into 20 small patties. It is easier to make 20 from the mixture if you first divide the mixture into 4 in the food processor bowl with a tablespoon and make 5 patties from each portion. Flatten them lightly in the middle and place on a plate.

›› Heat the oil in a saucepan. The oil is ready when the sulphur free end of a matchstick fizzes when dipped into the oil. Fry half of the falafel patties at a time at high heat in the oil for 2-4 minutes, until golden brown. If the oil is too hot they turn brown quickly, but are not entirely cooked through. Leave to drain on a piece of kitchen roll.

! The mixture can also be used for making 'burgers' for falafel burgers. See page 177.

Firm

33

SUSHI ROLLS

Sushi, surely that is something with raw fish? NO, sushi is in fact rice which has been marinated with vinegar and sugar. If the rice has been cooked in the correct amount of water for the right time and then marinated, it tastes delicious whether it is real sushi rice, white – or brown – rice or pudding rice. You can also use quinoa. You can use rice vinegar or just ordinary vinegar for the marinade. You really can't go wrong. Sushi always tastes delicious and is light on the stomach.

! See exciting sushi fillings on page 36-37.

With salad and avocado

Pickled sushi-ginger

With mango

With asparagus

Soy sauce

Wasabi

Inside out

Rice or quinoa

Makes 8 medium rolls or 4-6 inside-out rolls.

500 ml sushi rice or pudding rice
800 ml water

or

400 ml short grain brown rice
800 ml water

or

400 ml whole quinoa
500 ml water

Marinade
Makes 1 portion rice or quinoa

5 tbsp rice vinegar
2½ tbsp sugar
1 tsp salt

For rolling
Rolling mat

For serving
soy sauce
wasabi
pickled sushi-ginger

>> Rinse the rice thoroughly. Boil the rice with the water, turn it down and leave to boil for 15 minutes under a lid. Remove the saucepan from the heat and leave the rice on the side for 10 minutes. Leave to cool a little.

>> Rinse the rice thoroughly and leave to drain. Bring the rice to the boil with the water, turn down to low heat and leave to simmer for 50 minutes.

>> Rinse the quinoa in a sieve. Boil the quinoa with the water, leave to boil for 10 minutes. Turn off the heat and leave the quinoa on the side for 10 minutes.

>> Warm the vinegar in a small saucepan and stir in sugar and salt without bringing to the boil, just until the sugar and salt have almost dissolved. Leave the marinade to cool.

>> Pour the cooled cooked rice into a large bowl. Mix the marinade thoroughly with the rice. Use a scraper for mixing the rice and make 'cutting movements' through the rice so the marinade is distributed and the rice becomes a little elastic.

>> Cover the rice with a damp cloth and leave to cool completely. The rice is now ready for rolling. It should not be put in the fridge.

>> Have a bowl of cold water ready for dipping your fingers in between rolling.

>> Place one sheet of nori with the smooth side down on the rolling mat, so the grooves follow the strings on the mat.

>> Arrange a ½ cm thick layer of rice on the seaweed so the sheet is covered apart from the ⅓ furthest away from you. Do not press the rice too firmly. Press 2-3 rice grains at the edge where there is no rice, they will act as a glue for the roll when you roll it up.

>> Spread a little wasabi paste, 2 tsp spice mayo or 2 tsp miso dressing in the middle of the rice.

>> Place the filling in the middle of the rice on top of the wasabi, spice mayo (page 36) or miso dressing (page 36).

>> Roll the seaweed and rice around the filling. Take the mat between your hands and press the roll lightly.

>> Roll the sushi roll out of the mat. Make all the rolls and slice at once.

>> Place the roll on a chopping board and cut into 1-1 ½ cm thick slices using a sharp knife. Dry the knife with a clean dishcloth between each cut to prevent rice building up on the sides of the sushi.

>> Serve the sushi rolls with small dishes of soy sauce and small blobs of wasabi. Whisk a little wasabi into the sauce with the chop sticks and dip the rolls in this mixture. Eat ginger in between to clean the palate.

Firm

SUSHI FILLINGS

The filling in the sushi rolls can be varied ad infinitum and it is always fun to serve several different types. These suggestions are given per roll so you can prepare the filling according to how many of each kind you want to make. Follow the method on page 35.

Spicy sushi roll with salad and avocado

Salad in sushi rolls will give a wonderfully crisp texture. Use the inner leaves from romaine lettuce and slice thinly lengthways. Cut the avocado into three pieces.

Per roll
1 sheet nori
1-2 leaves romaine lettuce
¼ avocado
2 tsp spicy mayo

Spicy mayo (for 5 rolls)
1 tbsp good quality mayonnaise
1 tbsp sambal oelek
1 tsp dark sesame oil
1 tbsp sweet chilli sauce

>> Mix the mayonnaise with sambal oelek, sesame oil and sweet chilli sauce.

Sushi roll with mango, sesame seeds and miso

Miso mixed with lime juice has a very special strong and lightly acidic flavour.

Per roll
1 sheet nori
Approx. ⅛ mango
1 tsp toasted sesame seeds
2 tsp finely cut spring onions
1-2 tsp miso dressing

Miso dressing (for 4-6 rolls)
1 tbsp miso, red if available
1 tbsp lime juice

>> Cut the mango into sticks of approx. 1½ x 1½ cm and as long as possible. Toast the sesame seeds in a dry frying pan until they are fragrant and begin to 'pop'.

Firm

Sushi rolls with asparagus, bean sprouts, cress and wasabi

Per roll
1 sheet nori
2-3 asparagus spears
1 small handful bean sprouts
1 tbsp cress
1 tsp wasabi

>> Boil the asparagus in lightly salted water for 3-4 minutes until tender, but still al dente. Leave to cool in cold water and drain. Pour the bean sprouts into a sieve and leave to drain.

Inside out with carrot, radish, avocado and sesame seeds

Per roll
1 sheet nori
2 tsp toasted sesame seeds
¼ carrot cut into thin sticks
3 radishes cut into thin sticks
¼ avocado, cut into three
1 tsp wasabi

>> Use twice as much rice compared to ordinary sushi rolls. Fill two thirds of the sheet of nori with rice. Cut the remainder off.

>> Sprinkle with sesame seeds and press lightly into the rice.

>> Place a piece of cling film over the rice and sesame seeds and turn the seaweed over.

>> Place a layer of rice on the other side and place the filling in the middle. Roll the sushi as before but take care that the cling film is not rolled up with the roll. Wrap the roll in the cling film.

>> Cut the sushi with the cling film so the rice does not stick to the knife and remove it from each piece afterwards.

! The world's quickest sushi: Put the marinated rice in individual bowls, cut the filling into small mouth-size bits and place on top of the rice. Drizzle with soy sauce and sprinkle with small bits of wasabi and pickled sushi-ginger. Eat with chop sticks from the bowl.

! Read about Japanese ingredients page 216-217.

Firm

The vegetable lover's everyday pie

This everyday pie is not like any other. Normally there is a lot of butter in the pastry and cream in the filling. This pastry is made from coarse flour which gives the base a biscuit-like crisp texture, and we use a minimum of fat. The filling is made with crème fraîche 18%, sour cream 9% or Greek yogurt which makes the filling a little creamier. You will quickly get used to this pie with a difference. This is how, in our opinion, a vegetable pie should be. Serve with a crisp salad.

Pastry
175 g plain white flour
50 g rye flour, wholegrain spelt
   flour or wholemeal flour
½ tsp salt
50 g butter
100 ml cold water

Filling
500 g broccoli
1 tbsp rapeseed or olive oil
1 red sweet pepper
200 g carrots
100 g red salad onion

Egg mixture
3 eggs
400 ml crème fraîche 18%,
   sour cream 9%, or Greek
   yogurt 10%
2-3 tsp curry powder
1 tbsp cornflour
100 ml milk
1 tsp salt
Freshly ground pepper

» Turn on the oven at 200C/gas 6. Mix the plain white flour with the coarse flour and the salt in a bowl. Cut the butter into small cubes and crumble into the flour mixture. Add water and knead the pastry quickly until it just coming away from the bowl.

» Using a rolling pin roll out the pastry on a floured surface and place in a pie dish of 24-26 cm diameter. Or press the pastry into the dish. Using a fork make holes in the bottom of the pie. Bake the pie in the oven for 10 minutes.

» Cut the broccoli into florets and the stalk into cubes. Remove the seeds and cut the sweet pepper into large cubes or strips. Fry quickly in a large frying pan in the oil for 5 minutes while continuing to stir.

» Whisk the eggs, cream or yogurt, curry powder, cornflour, milk, salt and pepper in a bowl. Grate the carrots coarsely and mix into the egg mixture.

» Place the fried vegetables over the pie base and pour the egg mixture over the vegetables. Cut the onion into thick slices and place between the vegetables.

» Turn the oven down to 180C/gas 4 and bake the pie for 20-30 minutes until the surface is golden brown and firm when pressed lightly.

! You can vary the filling ad infinitum and just use what is in your fridge. You will need 1 kg vegetables, (unprepared) for the pie. The most suitable vegetables are mushrooms, leeks, broccoli, sweet peppers, courgette, onion, fennel and tomatoes. You can use other grated root vegetables apart from carrot – celeriac, parsnip, Hamburg parsley and beetroot are all suitable.

! You do not need to fry the vegetables. The pie will also be delicious even if you place the vegetables raw on the pre-baked base. You will need 800 g raw vegetables (unprepared).

! Try also to vary the flavouring for the egg mixture. Choose from:
- 2-3 tsp curry powder, paprika, oregano or tarragon or 1-2 tsp dried chilli flakes
- 50 ml-100 ml fresh, chopped herbs, dill, chives, thyme, basil, tarragon or parsley
- 2 tbsp tomato puree
- 2 tbsp red or green pesto

Firm

! Make mushroom-cheese burgers by adding 4 tbsp cornflour to the mixture. Makes 12 burgers using 2½ heaped tbsp of the mixture. Place in a hot frying pan with oil. Flatten out to make them approx. 1½ cm high. Turn down the heat to medium and continue frying for approx. 8 minutes on each side until firm, brown and crisp. Add a slice of cheese to each burger for the remaining 4 minutes.

! The mixture is also delicious as burgers for a packed lunch. Make the number of burgers you will eat for your evening meal and then make small burgers with the rest of the mixture for packed lunches. Fry in oil using 1 tbsp of the mixture for 2-3 minutes on each side. They are ready when they are brown, firm and crisp.

Warm mushroom-walnut pâté

Some readers may remember our recipe for warm mushroom pâté. This is an updated version, spicy and not quite as fatty and using quinoa instead of rice. Serve with spinach sauce e.g. page 112 and a crisp salad.

1 whole quinoa (300 ml boiled)
175 ml water
50 g walnuts
1 tbsp olive oil + for brushing
300 g onions
500 g mixed mushrooms
1 clove garlic, pressed
3 tbsp chopped fresh tarragon (or 1 tbsp dried)
2 eggs
100 ml Greek yogurt 10% fat
1½ tsp salt
Freshly ground pepper

>> Rinse the quinoa in cold water in a sieve. Boil in a pan under a lid with the water for 10 minutes, remove from the heat, add salt and set aside with the lid on top for 10 minutes. Leave the quinoa to cool.

>> Chop the walnuts coarsely. Toast the nuts in a dry, hot pan until golden. Shake the pan during cooking.

>> Peel and chop the onions finely. Remove any soil from the mushrooms with kitchen towel. Chop the mushrooms finely. Fry the onions in oil at a high temperature for approx. 5 minutes, continue to stir, add the mushrooms and continue to fry for a further approx. 10 minutes, until the mushrooms are dry and toasted.

>> Remove the mushrooms from the heat, add to a bowl and mix with quinoa, walnuts, pressed garlic, tarragon, eggs, yogurt, salt and pepper.

>> Add the mixture to an ovenproof dish approx. 15 x 20 cm, brushed with a little oil. The mixture is approx. 3 cm high – if it is higher it will need a little longer to cook.

>> Bake in the oven at 180C/gas 4 for approx. 30 minutes, until the pâté is firm when pressed lightly.

Root vegetables PANCAKES

Serve these with smoked cheese raw salad, page 83, a portion of tzatziki page 98, or a salad of bitter leaves which will be a good contrast to the slightly sweeter root vegetables, e.g. endive, frisée or beet leaves.

Makes approx. 20

200 g celeriac and or/parsnip
200 g carrot and or/parsnip
½ leek, bottom or top
2 eggs
120 g coarse flour, e.g. rye
   flour, wholemeal flour or
   coarse spelt flour
Approx. 250 ml milk
1 tsp salt
Freshly ground pepper
2 tsp fresh thyme leaves or
   1 tsp dried thyme
Neutral tasting oil
Or olive oil, for frying

›› Peel and rinse the root vegetables and the leek and cut them into large chunks.

›› Add vegetables and eggs, flour, milk, salt, pepper and thyme to a food processor and blend to a thick mixture.

›› Heat 2 tsp oil in a frying pan and shape 4 small pancakes at a time. Use approx. 2 tbsp of the mixture and smooth the surface with the spoon. Fry the pancakes until golden on medium heat on one side, turn over and fry at a slightly lower heat on the other side until golden. Drizzle, if necessary with 1 tsp oil when turning over.

›› Keep warm in a dish in the oven until all the pancakes have been cooked.

! Fresh thyme will give a good, strong flavour which is excellent with all dishes using root vegetables and emphasises the flavour of autumn and winter vegetables. A quick way of picking the leaves from the stalk is by holding the thyme stalk at the root end and 'tearing' the leaves off by pulling in the opposite direction.

POTATO pancakes

Serve these potato pancakes with e.g. a cucumber radish-smoked cheese cream, page 97, smoked raw salad page 83 or tzatziki page 98. Or serve with cottage cheese mixed with pressed garlic or finely chopped chives.

Makes 10-20 depending on the size

1 kg potatoes
200 g onions
½ tsp caraway seeds (optional)
2 eggs
6 tbsp plain white flour
1 tsp salt
Freshly ground pepper
Rapeseed oil for frying

▶▶ Peel the potatoes and grate them coarsely. Squeeze almost all of the water out of the potatoes using your hands. Put the grated potatoes into a bowl.

▶▶ Peel and grate the onions coarsely. If using, chop the caraway seeds a little using a knife on a chopping board.

▶▶ Mix potatoes thoroughly with the onions, caraway seeds, eggs, flour, salt and pepper.

▶▶ Heat 2-3 tsp rapeseed oil at a time in a frying pan and using a tablespoon shape 2-4 pancakes approx. ½ cm high. They should fill the entire pan without touching each other but do not need to be perfectly round. Smooth the surface with the spoon. Fry at medium heat and turn over when golden brown. Fry until golden brown also on the other side, drizzle if necessary with 1 extra tsp oil during cooking.

▶▶ Place the pancakes in a serving dish while you make the next lot. You will make 10-20 pancakes from the mixture, depending on whether you make 2 large or 4 smaller ones at a time.

Firm

Potato pancakes

Cucumber smoked cheese creamy

I did not become vegetarian for the sake of my health. I became vegetarian for the sake of the health of chickens.
Isaac Bashevis Singer, writer

Fennel-bean MUFFINS

Serve these muffins hot or warm with a mixed green salad, using an olive oil and balsamic dressing.

Makes 12

250 g dried white beans
(550 g boiled)
½ tsp fennel seeds, 1 clove
  garlic, 1 bayleaf and vegetable
  stock for boiling
200 ml milk
300 g carrots
2 eggs
2 tbsp plain white flour
½ tsp fennel seeds
1-2 garlic cloves
1½ tsp salt
Freshly ground pepper

Topping

125 g grated cheddar cheese
15-18 cherry tomatoes, or more
A little olive oil
Fresh basil, for garnish

Paper muffin cases or metal
  muffin tins lined with baking
  paper

>> Start the day before by soaking the beans in double the amount of water or more.

>> When ready to cook pour away the water and rinse the beans thoroughly. Boil with coarsely chopped fennel seeds, garlic, bayleaf and plenty of vegetable stock under a lid for approx. 1-1 ¼ hours until cooked through and soft.

>> Drain the beans and mash in a bowl with a hand blender or in a food processor with the milk until the beans have become pureed.

>> Peel and grate the carrots coarsely on a vegetable grater and mix with the bean puree with eggs, flour, coarsely chopped fennel seeds, pressed garlic, salt and pepper.

>> Place the mixture in 10-12 muffin tins. Sprinkle the cheese on top of the muffins. Cut the tomatoes into halves and place on top of the cheese, drizzle with a little oil and sprinkle with salt and pepper.

>> Bake in the oven at 200C/gas 6 for approx. 35 minutes until golden and firm when pressed lightly.

! Grated cheese from a leftover bit from the fridge can be used instead of cheddar and you can use any kind of tomato.

! Use a larger portion of tomatoes as we have done in the photo for serving but not in the recipe.

Firm

47

POLENTA

Polenta is a kind of porridge made of coarse cornflour. In Northern Italy there is a tradition of eating polenta instead of pasta but with the same sauces which are used for pasta. Polenta is easy to make and you can make a portion which will keep for several days and vary it by serving it freshly made the first day, and steamed, fried or grilled the next few times. Polenta is lovely and light on the stomach and is also gluten free. Use 'minute polenta' which is pre-boiled corn grain which only needs 5 minutes cooking. Always use a saucepan which is big enough to avoid the porridge spilling up over the edge during cooking.

1 litre water
2 tsp salt
250 g minute polenta
1 tbsp chopped fresh thyme
3 tbsp freshly grated parmesan
   (optional)

>> Boil the water with salt. Remove the saucepan from the heat and sprinkle the polenta flour into the pot little by little while whisking, continue to whisk briskly.

>> Replace the pan on the heat and turn down the heat to a lower temperature. Change the whisk and now use a wooden spoon. Mix thoroughly and add thyme. Leave the porridge to simmer under a lid for 5 minutes. Stir the porridge now and then to avoid it burning. It may stick to the bottom of the pan in a thin layer but that will not affect the quality. Leave the saucepan to soak after cooking for ½ hour then it will be easier to clean.

>> Add parmesan and season to taste. Serve immediately.

Steamed, fried or grilled polenta

Put the freshly boiled porridge in a small square dish or a plastic box with high edges. Leave it to set, this will take approx. 1 hour. In the fridge, it will now keep for a couple of days.
Turn the set polenta onto a chopping board and cut into slices, blocks, triangles, rounds or any shape you want. Fry the polenta until golden in olive oil in a frying pan. Or brush it with a little olive oil on all sides and cook on a griddle or ridged grill pan until they have a beautiful hatched pattern. Or put them in an oven proof dish with a little water and cover with foil. Heat the polenta in the oven at 200C/gas 6 for 15 minutes. Serve with the same sauces as if it was freshly cooked.

! If you have been unable to find the minute polenta and are using ordinary polenta or coarse cornflour, the porridge should boil for approx. 45-50 minutes.

! Add parmesan and fresh herbs to the polenta to taste. Serve the freshly made polenta in soup plates with spinach sauce page 112, mushroom sauce page 109, tomato sauce page 113 or tex mex hot pot page 156.

Firm

Grilled polenta

Spinach sauce
page 112

Steamed polenta

WRAPPED

flat breads with fillings and toppings

! How do you easily measure $\frac{1}{12}$ of a large portion of vegetables? Divide the vegetables at the bottom of the pan with your wooden spoon by scraping each part a little up the sides of the pan and making a gap in the middle. Divide each half into two. Now you can work out approx. how much of each quarter makes up a third that should go into each spring roll.

This chapter contains recipes for rolls, packed meals, pizzas, pancakes and wraps i.e. crisp pastry with delicious fillings. They can either be a main course, lunch or first course.

SPRING rolls

Serve spring rolls with a raw salad or crisp salad, with Asian flavour elements.

Makes 12

6 sheets filo pastry
300 g pointed cabbage or white cabbage
2 leeks
200 g carrots
250 g fresh mushrooms or dried and soaked if necessary
150 g bean sprouts or vegetables of your choice
2 cloves garlic, pressed through garlic press
1½ tsp 5-spice (optional)
2 tbsp dry sherry or rice wine
3 tbsp soy sauce
4 tbsp water
2 tsp sugar
2 tsp salt
1 tbsp cornflour
Neutral tasting oil for frying

Serve with

Soy sauce
Chilli sauce, e.g. Tabasco or sambal oelek
Sweet chilli sauce

>> If frozen, defrost the filo pastry according to the instructions on the packet.

>> Slice the cabbage finely. Cut the leeks into slices of ½ cm. Peel the carrots and grate them coarsely. Clean the mushrooms and chop them roughly. Rinse the bean sprouts in a sieve and leave to drain.

>> Fry the vegetables in 2 tbsp oil in a hot wok, large frying pan or saucepan. Fry half the vegetables at a time in half of the oil each time, as it is a rather large portion. Fry at high heat for approx. 5 minutes until the vegetables have wilted a little, but are still crisp. Stir the vegetables frequently to avoid them burning. Add pressed garlic and 5-spice, (optional).

>> Mix sherry or rice wine, soy sauce, water, sugar and salt in a bowl and mix in the cornflour. Pour this mixture over the vegetables all at once. Cook continuing to stir until the sauce thickens and then leave to cool at room temperature.

>> Unroll the filo pastry carefully. Take one sheet at a time. Cover the rest of the pastry with a damp tea towel. Cut the sheet in the middle of the short part. Place ¹/₁₂ of the vegetables at the end of one piece of pastry. Fold the pastry over the filling and roll the pastry round the filling. Repeat with the rest of the spring roll. Place on a serving dish and cover with cling film until ready to cook.

>> To serve: Fry the spring rolls in plenty of oil at high temperature until golden and crisp on all sides. Leave to drain on kitchen roll.

>> Serve the spring rolls with soy sauce, hot chilli sauce or sambal oelek and sweet chilli sauce and salad or raw vegetables.

! The spring rolls can also be baked in the oven on a sheet lined with baking paper at 200C/gas 6 for 10-15 minutes. Brush the pastry with neutral tasting oil on the inside before adding the filling and on the outside when they have been rolled up. This will make them crisp in a different, good way and much less fattening.

! Instead of filo pastry you can use spring roll pastry available frozen from Asian shops. Here you can also buy 5-spice, a mixture of ground spices which is typically made from cinnamon, star anise, ginger and cloves.

Filo parcels with WINTER FILLING

The vegetarian's Christmas or winter food. Serve these filo packets with the nut sauce below and the celery cream with fresh goat's cheese page 92 or creamy potatoes with turnips page 134.

Makes 8

4 sheets filo pastry
450 g Jerusalem artichokes
200 g shallots or onions
250 g mushrooms, e.g. shiitake, oyster caps and field mushrooms
2 tbsp butter
2 apples
150 g prunes without stones
1½ tsp fennel seeds
1½ tsp coriander seeds
2 tbsp peeled, freshly grated ginger
Juice of 2 oranges
Salt
Freshly ground pepper
50 g butter or 2-3 tbsp neutral tasting oil for brushing
1 egg, beaten

≫ If frozen, defrost the filo pastry according to the instructions on the packet.

≫ Scrub the Jerusalem artichokes thoroughly with a vegetable brush or peel them. Cut them into ½ cm thin slices. Peel the onions and cut them in ½ cm thin slices lengthways. Clean the mushrooms and cut into halves. Oyster caps may be torn into large chunks.

≫ Fry the onions and Jerusalem artichokes in the butter in a sauce-pan over medium heat for 4-5 minutes while continuing to stir. Add the mushrooms and fry until everything has turned a light golden colour.

≫ Remove the core from the apple and cut each apple into 8 sections. Grind fennel seeds and coriander seeds in a mortar. Mix apples, prunes, fennel, coriander and ginger with the other ingredients in a saucepan. Heat everything thoroughly and add orange juice, salt and pepper to taste.

≫ Melt 50 g butter over a low heat in a saucepan. Unroll the filo pastry carefully. Take one sheet of pastry at a time. Cover the rest of the pastry with a damp tea towel. Cut the sheet in the middle of the short part. Brush one piece with butter or oil and place the other one on top. Place ⅛ of the filling in the middle of the pastry. Brush around the filling with egg which will act as the 'glue'. Draw the pastry up around the filling and press it together lightly.

≫ Place the parcel on a baking sheet lined with baking paper and brush with the egg mixture but only below the opening. Then make the next parcel in the same way.

≫ To serve: Bake in the oven at 180C/gas 4 for approx. 20 minutes, until golden and crisp.

! The parcels can be made in advance. Place on a tray, cover with cling film and leave in the fridge until ready to bake.

Nut sauce

100 g hazelnuts
50 ml hazelnut oil or neutral tasting oil
2 tsp freshly chopped thyme
A pinch of salt

≫ Brown the nuts in the oven at 200C/gas 6 for 10-15 minutes until fragrant and the skins are loosening. Leave to cool a little and then rub off the skins.

≫ Blend the nuts with the oil in a mini chopper or use a pole blender but take care that they do not become too finely chopped.

Mix the thyme and salt with the sauce and season to taste.

Summer FILO PARCELS with asparagus

Serve with smoked cheese raw salad page 83 or tzatziki page 98.

Makes 6

500 g green asparagus
600 g boiled potatoes
2 tbsp freshly chopped thyme
2 tsp finely grated organic lemon
   peel
Salt and freshly ground pepper
6 sheets filo pastry
50 g melted butter or oil for
   brushing
1 egg

>> Break off the woody end of the asparagus and boil in lightly salted water for 3 minutes. Leave to cool in cold water and drain in a sieve. Cut the asparagus into 1 cm slices.

>> Cut the potatoes into 1 x 1 cm cubes and mix with the asparagus, thyme, lemon peel, salt and pepper. Then continue using the same method as for the winter vegetable parcels.

Filo parcel with
winter filling and
nut sauce

VEGETABLE PIZZAS

Make any of the toppings you fancy. See page 58.

Makes 4 pizzas

Pastry
25 g fresh yeast
400 ml lukewarm water
1 tsp salt
2 tsp olive oil
200 g coarse spelt flour
400 g durum flour (grano duro)

>> Dissolve the yeast in the water. Add salt and olive oil, spelt flour and most of the durum flour and knead the dough. Add more durum flour while kneading, until the dough is soft and firm and just slips off your fingers. Cover and leave the dough to rise for approx. 30 minutes.

>> Heat the oven at 240C/gas 9. Heat a baking tray at the bottom of the oven.

>> Divide the dough into 4. Roll each ball of dough out on a sheet of baking paper (or roll it on a table covered with a little flour, or press the dough out onto the baking paper) to form a circle of approx. 26 cm diameter.

>> Add filling and place the baking paper with the pizza onto the warm baking sheet and bake for 8-10 minutes until the cheese has melted and the base is golden brown at the edge.

Variation
The pizza may also be rolled out to a bigger circle which makes it thinner. You can also roll 2 pieces of the dough to form a square which fills the entire baking sheet; then it will be a real family pizza and everyone will be served at the same time. The fillings could be placed in separate areas so there is something for everyone in the same pizza.

! If you do not use all the dough, it will keep in a plastic box in the fridge until the following day. This is what they do in pizzerias.

Tomato sauce

Makes 4 pizzas

100 g tin peeled tomatoes
1 small tin (70 g) concentrated
   tomato puree
2 cloves garlic
1 tsp salt

>> Blend the tomatoes with tomato puree, garlic and salt.

Cheese

Use any ordinary hard cheese, which you grate on the rough side of the grater. Or you can grate mozzarella also on the coarse side of the grater. It looks a little strange, but it works better grated than cut into slices, when it will not be distributed evenly over the pizza. In Italy there is a heated debate about whether mozzarella is at all suitable for pizza. Grated mozzarella or any cooking cheese works well too.

Potato and Nigella

Broccoli and olive

Spinach and
artichoke

Cut the finished pizza with
scissors. It is easier than cutting
it with a knife.

Mushrooms and
gorgonzola

Toppings

The portions are enough for 1 pizza (see photo page 57).

Mushrooms and gorgonzola

4 tbsp tomato sauce
150 g mushrooms e.g. button, chanterelles, ceps, shiitake or oyster caps
50 g gorgonzola
2 tsp dried oregano

>> Spread the tomato sauce over the pizza base.

>> Clean the mushrooms. Slice and distribute evenly over the base.

>> Break the gorgonzola into very tiny pieces and distribute over the base. Sprinkle with oregano.

Broccoli, olive and chilli

150 g broccoli
4 tbsp tomato sauce
75 g grated cheese or ½ grated mozzarella
25 g small black olives
Chilli flakes

>> Cut the broccoli into florets and cut the stalk into cubes or slices. Lightly boil the broccoli in lightly salted water, leave to cool in cold water and drain in a sieve. Cut the florets into smaller pieces.

>> Spread the tomato sauce evenly over the base. Sprinkle the cheese evenly over the base. Place broccoli and olives evenly on top of the tomato sauce and cheese and sprinkle with chilli flakes.

Spinach and artichoke

150 g fresh spinach
2 tsp olive oil
1 clove garlic, finely chopped
Salt
2-3 artichoke hearts
75 g grated cheese or ½ grated mozzarella
Chilli flakes (optional)

>> Clean the spinach thoroughly in plenty of cold water and leave to drain. Heat the oil in a saucepan and lightly fry the spinach until it wilts. Mix the finely chopped garlic with the spinach, add salt to taste and continue frying until any liquid has evaporated. Place the spinach evenly over the pizza base.

>> Cut the artichoke hearts into quarters and distribute evenly over the base. Sprinkle the cheese and chilli flakes, if using, over the filling.

Potato, Nigella and rosemary

4 tbsp tomato sauce
Approx. 75 g grated cheese or ½ mozzarella
150 g peeled potatoes
1-2 tsp olive oil
¼ tsp salt
2 tsp dried rosemary
2 tsp Nigella seeds

>> Spread the tomato sauce over the pizza base. Sprinkle the cheese over the base.

>> Cut the potatoes into very thin slices. Place the potato slices over the base but not on top of each other.

>> Drizzle with olive oil and sprinkle with salt and rosemary and/or Nigella seeds.

>> Variation: Use truffle oil instead of olive oil and leave out rosemary and Nigella. Sprinkle with 2 tbsp parmesan shavings and a handful rocket when the pizza is cooked.

Green cabbage

Spelt pancake

Horseradish cream

SPELT pancakes

Serve spelt pancakes with green cabbage salad page 83 and horseradish cream page 108.

Makes 8 small pancakes

120 g (200 ml) coarse spelt
  flour
2 eggs
¼ tsp salt
2 tbsp finely chopped parsley
  or chives
250 ml milk
Approx. 1 ½ tbsp neutral
  tasting oil for frying

>> Whisk spelt flour, eggs, salt and chopped parsley or chives. Add a little milk at a time until you have a light batter.

>> Heat a little oil at a time using a small frying pan. Use little more than 50 ml of the batter per pancake. Fry the pancakes until golden brown on both sides.

>> Keep the pancakes warm on a plate under foil in the oven.

>> To serve: Fold the green cabbage salad inside the pancakes and serve with horseradish cream

Wrapped

CHICKPEA pancakes

A non-stick frying pan is best for cooking chickpea pancakes. Serve as here with potato-spinach masala page 133 and raita page 96.

Makes 8 pancakes

400 ml chickpea (gram) flour
1½ tsp salt
500 ml water
2 tbsp neutral tasting oil
4 tsp Nigella seeds

➤➤ Add flour and salt to a bowl, whisk in the water a little at a time to make the batter light and without lumps. Add the oil. Leave the batter to rest for 15-30 minutes at room temperature; this will make it a little thicker.

➤➤ Whisk in a little more water. Add Nigella seeds.

➤➤ Cook medium sized pancakes over high heat in a non-stick frying pan without fat or oil. Use 75 ml of batter for each pancake. Turn pancake over when it is light brown and cook on the other side. Place on a plate and cover with foil. Make the rest in the same manner.

! You can use sesame seeds instead of Nigella seeds. Stir the batter each time you pour some into the pan to distribute the seeds evenly.

! Chickpea (gram) flour and Nigella seeds are available from ethnic shops.

Vegan jokes
How do you keep milk fresh?
By leaving it inside the cow.

Potato-spinach
masála

Raita

Tortilla wraps with BEAN mash

Wraps may be eaten with hot tomato dip page 108 and corn on the cob.

Makes 4 large or 8 small wholegrain wraps

250 g dried kidney beans
5 cloves garlic, 3 sprigs of fresh
    thyme, rosemary or sage or 2
    tsp dried and vegetable stock
    for cooking
1 tbsp cumin seeds
2 tsp fennel seeds
200 g onions
2 cloves garlic
1 tbsp olive oil
1 tsp finely grated organic orange
    peel
4 tbsp orange juice
Chilli sauce – powder or flakes
Salt

Filling
½ crisp lettuce, iceberg or
    romaine
200 g cabbage
2 carrots
½ cucumber
1 bunch fresh coriander

Packet of tortillas

>> Soak the beans overnight in plenty of cold water.

>> Discard the water used for soaking. Boil the beans with the whole garlic cloves, thyme, rosemary- or sage sprigs in plenty of vegetable stock. Leave the beans to simmer under a lid until tender and soft. Save approx. 200 ml of the water and discard the rest. Meanwhile prepare the rest of the ingredients.

>> Toast the cumin and fennel seeds in a pan while stirring until fragrant. Grind in a mortar.

>> Peel the onions and chop them coarsely. Slice the garlic or press using a garlic press.   Quickly fry the onions and garlic in the oil in the saucepan. Add the ground spices. Turn down the heat and leave the onions to simmer until clear and tender – stir now and then to avoid them burning.

>> Mix in the cooked beans, turn up the heat and fry quickly.

>> Blend the beans and onions with orange peel – and juice - and add a little of the water from the beans to make the mash soft enough for blending. Add chilli and salt to taste.

>> Filling: Slice the lettuce and the cabbage finely. Peel and cut the carrots into fine sticks. Cut the cucumber into fine sticks. Heat the tortilla wraps as indicated on the packet.

>> To serve: Spread the bean mash in the middle of the warm wrap, fill with crisp vegetables, sprinkle with coarsely chopped coriander and close the wrap. Eat with hot tomato dip and corn on the cob.

! You can also make the bean mash with 2 tins of kidney beans. Pour the juice away and fry the beans with the onions. Add water or vegetable stock when blending.

Vietnamese SUMMER ROLLS

You can make these rolls just before serving or 1-2 hours before but you can also wrap them in cling film and serve them the next day. Serve one or more dips with the summer rolls.   Choose either peanut sauce or hoisin sauce and either sweet chilli sauce or lemon grass sauce.

Makes 20 large rolls

1 lettuce, e.g. romaine,
    butterhead or iceberg
1 small bunch mint
1 bunch fresh coriander
800 g cleaned vegetables, 3-4
    different types, see tip
20 large round sheets rice paper

Sauces and dips
see page 68

>> Rinse and dry the lettuce. Wash and pick the mint and coriander.

>> Cut carrot, cucumber, Chinese radish, sugar snaps and sweet pepper into thin strips 5-6 cm long. If you are using avocado and/or mango cut these into thin slivers. Rinse bean sprouts in cold water and drain in a sieve. Break off the woody part of the asparagus, boil in lightly salted water until tender but still al dente, leave to cool and drain.

>> Place 3-4 pieces of rice paper in a large bowl of cold water and leave for a couple of minutes until pliable but not too soft.

>> Take one piece of softened rice paper at a time, drain a little and place on the work surface. Put a lettuce leaf in the middle of the rice paper overlapping the edge a little, then a small handful of vegetables, a couple of mint leaves and a few sprigs of coriander.

>> Fold the rice paper in the middle to cover the filling and roll the pastry around the filling from one side towards the other. Continue in this way with the rest of the rice papers and the filling.

>> Serve the summer rolls next to each other in a serving dish. Serve with one or several types of dips in small bowls.

! You can use a mixture of crisp and soft/juicy vegetables. The crisp ones: Carrots, Chinese radish, sugar snaps, sweet pepper, cucumber and bean sprouts. The soft/juicy: Avocado, asparagus and mango.

Peanut butter sauce

For 10 rolls

100 ml peanut butter
1 clove garlic, pressed through
   garlic press
1½ tbsp finely grated fresh
   ginger
2 tbsp soy sauce
2 tbsp sweet chilli sauce
5 tbsp water
¼ tsp cayenne pepper
4 tbsp freshly squeezed lemon/
   lime juice

>> Mix the peanut butter with pressed garlic and finely grated ginger, add soy sauce and chilli sauce.

>> Add a little water and season to taste with cayenne and lemon- or lime juice.

Hoisin coconut sauce

For 10 rolls

3 tbsp hoisin sauce
2 tbsp soy sauce
3 tbsp freshly squeezed lemon/
   lime juice
2 cloves garlic, pressed through
   garlic press
200 ml coconut milk
1 tsp sugar
½ tsp chilli powder or 1 tsp
   sambal oelek
2 tbsp chopped peanuts (optional)

>> Mix the hoisin sauce with soy sauce, lemon-or lime juice, pressed garlic and coconut milk. Add sugar and chilli to taste.

>> Sprinkle with chopped peanuts on top, (optional).

Lemon grass-chilli dip

For 10 rolls

1 lemon grass
1 small chilli
1 clove garlic
1 tsp sugar
3 tbsp lime juice
1 tbsp soy sauce

>> Remove the outer coarse part of the lemon grass and slice the bottom two thirds finely. Cut the chilli in half, remove the seeds and chop finely. Chop the garlic finely.

>> Mix lemon grass, chilli and garlic with sugar, lime juice and soy sauce and season to taste.

! The special ingredients are available from supermarkets or Asian shops. Sweet chilli sauce is also available in a bottle.

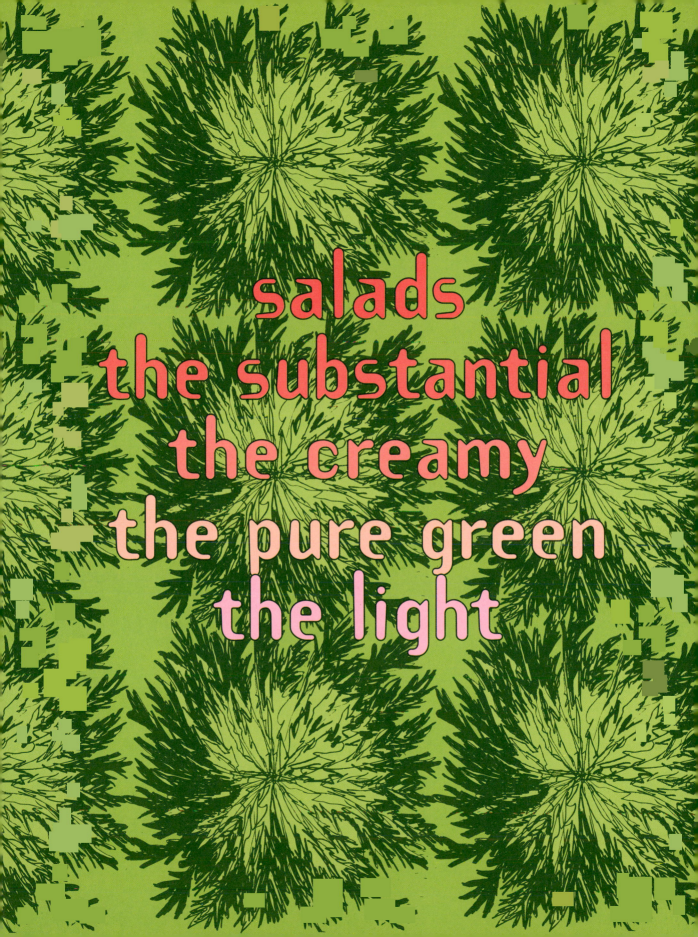

salads
the substantial
the creamy
the pure green
the light

Of course we have to include a chapter with best salads ever. These are arranged in four categories which complement each other both in texture and nutrition.

The substantial SALADS

Substantial salads contain a lot of fibrous carbohydrates which are very filling.

Buckwheat noodles with CRISP vegetables and sesame mayo

This is a pasta salad with a difference using beautiful light brown buckwheat noodles and coarse, raw vegetables. To make the coarse vegetables more fun to eat in large quantities it is worth the effort of cutting them really finely. It might take a little time to begin with but with practice it gets very easy. You can also grate carrots and radishes on a vegetable grater.

100 g buckwheat noodles
250 g pointed cabbage
1 carrot
1 bunch radishes
2 spring onions
1 sheet nori seaweed
2 tbsp cress

Dressing
50 ml good quality mayonnaise
1 tbsp dark sesame oil
4 tbsp lemon juice
¼ tsp cayenne pepper
salt

>> Boil the buckwheat noodles in lightly salted water as indicated on the packet but check regularly – they should be tender but still al dente. Drain and leave to cool in cold water.

>> Cut the cabbage finely. Cut the carrot and radishes into thin sticks. This is easiest by cutting them into thin slices, place the slices in a heap and cut the sticks into the same width as the slices are thick. Slice the spring onions across thinly.

>> Mix the mayonnaise with the sesame oil. Whisk in the lemon juice a little at a time to avoid the mayonnaise curdling. Add salt and cayenne pepper to taste.

>> Rinse the noodles in a little cold water just before serving or they might stick together. Arrange the noodles on a large serving dish. Mix the cabbage in with the noodles. Sprinkle with carrots, radishes and spring onions.

>> Pour the dressing over the salad and leave for 10-15 minutes.

>> Finally sprinkle with finely cut seaweed and cress.

! Make a winter version and use a lot of finely cut green cabbage instead of pointed cabbage.

Sliced

72

Mung bean salad with PINEAPPLE and chilli lime dressing

Mung beans are a positive surprise, both in terms of flavour and because they need very little cooking time. The beans do not have to be soaked. The salad also tastes delicious as a complete meal served with hot or warm rice.

200 g dried mung beans
1 clove garlic, 1 tsp cumin seeds
   and vegetable stock for boiling
50 g walnuts
1 large or 2 small avocadoes
300 g fresh pineapple, peeled
250 g red sweet pepper
1 handful chopped fresh mint

Chilli lime dressing

½ tsp cumin seeds
½ - 1 red chilli
3 tbsp freshly squeezed lime
   juice
2 tsp maple syrup
salt

▶▶ Rinse the beans and boil them with coarsely chopped garlic, cumin and plenty of vegetable stock for 15-20 minutes until tender. Keep an eye on them as they will suddenly become mushy. When they are al dente, remove from the heat and leave on one side for a couple of minutes before draining the water. You can serve them lukewarm.

▶▶ Toast the nuts in a dry, hot pan. Chop coarsely. Put aside for later.

▶▶ Toast the cumin seeds on a very hot frying pan until fragrant while shaking the pan all the time. Crush lightly in a mortar. Cut the chilli in half, lengthwise, remove the seeds and membranes. Cut or chop the chilli finely. Mix cumin seeds and chilli with lime juice and maple syrup to make the dressing. Add salt to taste.

▶▶ Cut avocado, pineapple and de-seeded pepper into small cubes and add to the dressing with the beans. Add salt, lime juice and syrup to taste.

▶▶ Garnish with mint and nuts.

Can a vegetarian eat meat-eating plants?
We have never heard the question before
and we do not know the answer, do you?

Bille's multi-bean salad

This salad is super easy, beautiful and colourful guest food that will be very popular. Bille makes it often using different types of boiled beans which she keeps in the freezer. She mixes fresh, crisp vegetables with the beans to give the floury contrast and adds a few boiled fresh ones to make it extra juicy. Vegetables with strong colours, green and red, e.g. tomatoes and sweet peppers go well with the black, white and brown beans. For extra flavour she adds something a little sharp tasting: Raw onions, fresh herbs, chilli, wine vinegar and garlic to give the salad an extra kick.

400 g boiled beans, several
  kinds and preferably different
  colours and sizes (you can
  also use tinned beans)
250 g green beans
2 sweet peppers, e.g. 1 red and
  1 yellow
1 red salad onion
1 bunch fresh basil, parsley,
  tarragon, oregano or marjoram,
  or 2 handfuls of rocket
Salt and freshly ground pepper

Dressing
2 cloves garlic
1 chilli
2 tbsp olive oil
2 tbsp white wine vinegar,
  sherry vinegar, 3 tbsp fresh
  lemon juice
Salt

›› First make the dressing: Chop the garlic finely. Cut the chilli length-ways, remove the seeds and membranes and chop the chilli finely. Whisk oil and vinegar or lemon juice with the garlic, chilli and salt.

›› Mix the boiled beans with the dressing and leave to absorb the dressing while you prepare the vegetables for the salad.

›› Pinch the stalk off the green beans and boil in lightly salted water for 3-5 minutes until tender and al dente. Leave to cool in cold water and drain. Cut into 2-3 cm pieces.

›› Remove the seeds from the sweet peppers and cut into small cubes. Chop the onion finely. Chop the herbs coarsely.

›› Mix red onion, green beans and herbs with the marinated beans and add salt and pepper and extra vinegar or lemon juice to taste.

Variation:
Everything in the salad has been cut into the same small cubes so you will have a little of everything with each mouthful. You can choose to make a more rustic salad with whole boiled green beans and sweet peppers sliced into thin rings or strips, a salad which may look better if arranged in a beautiful serving dish. But for flavour it is a different experience.

! To make sure the beans absorb the flavour from the dressing it is a good idea to leave the beans to marinate for up to 1 hour. Only add the green beans just before serving as they turn grey from the acid in the dressing.

The PURE green salads

Vegetables with lots of fibre is the code word for the following salads.

Baked ROOT vegetables with favourite variations

Baked root vegetables taste fantastic. Perhaps you bake root vegetables now and then and serve them hot, lukewarm or cold as a salad. We have collected an ideas bank with variations for you to choose from. Choose an oil, add salt and one or more spices to taste. Or bake the root vegetables with fresh herbs and combine with seeds or nuts. Or sprinkle the baked root vegetables with fresh herbs, raw onions or horseradish. Experiment and find your favourite combinations.

1 ¼ kg root vegetables, e.g. beetroot, parsnip, celeriac, Hamburg parsley, carrot or kohlrabi
1 tbsp olive oil or cold pressed rapeseed oil
Salt

Ideas bank for variations

Spices, choose from: 1 tbsp lightly crushed fennel seeds, 1 tbsp lightly crushed coriander, 1 tbsp lightly crushed cumin seeds, 1½ tbsp garam masala or curry powder, 2 tbsp tandoori spice mix or 1 tsp smoked paprika.

1 small bunch fresh herbs which you bake with the vegetables, choose from: Sage, rosemary, thyme or lovage.

Seeds which you sprinkle over the root vegetables and bake with them to make them crisp, choose from: 1 tbsp Nigella, 1 tbsp flax seeds, 2 tbsp sunflower seeds, 2 tbsp poppy seeds or 2 tbsp sesame seeds.

For acidic taste to mix with the root vegetables after baking, choose from: 2 tbsp lemon-or lime juice, 2 tbsp cider vinegar, 2 tbsp berry vinegar, 1½ tbsp sherry vinegar, 1½ tbsp red- or white wine vinegar, 2 tbsp red or white balsamic vinegar.

Fresh, coarsely chopped herbs for mixing with the root vegetables after baking. Choose a handful from: Parsley, tarragon, lovage, chives, basil, dill, or coriander.

Other flavour enhancers which can be sprinkled over the baked root vegetables, choose from: Grated peel of 1 organic lemon or orange, 3-4 tbsp grated horseradish or 1 small finely chopped raw onion.

›› Peel the root vegetables. Cut into any shape or size you want. Find your favourite or alternate a little each time — that will give you variation. Large and thick slices will give a rustic appearance. Thin strips are more elegant and quicker to cook. Choose from: Cubes, any type of shape, sticks, boats, and slices.

›› Place in a plastic bag and shake with olive oil and spices.

›› Place on a baking tray lined with baking paper and make sure they do not overlap — preferably just one layer. Sprinkle with seeds or one or several of the fresh herbs.

›› Bake at 200C/gas 6 until tender but still al dente. The cooking time will depend on the thickness of the root vegetables.

›› After cooking add vinegars, lemon juice and/or herbs and/or any other flavour enhancers.

›› Serve hot, lukewarm or cold.

! Onions and leeks can be cut into suitable slices and baked with the root vegetables. Garlic can be chopped finely and added for the last 5-10 minutes of the cooking time.

Parsnip with curry powder

Beetroot with tandoori spice mix

Celeriac with lovage

Carrots with Nigella

SEAWEED salad with crisp vegetables

Edamame, (e-da-ma-me) are green soy beans in their pod which are available frozen and sometimes without their pod. You do not eat the pod. The salad also tastes delicious as a complete meal served with hot or lukewarm rice.

3 small handfuls (15 g) dried seaweed, arame and/or wakame
1 tbsp soy sauce
1 clove garlic, pressed through garlic press
400 g edamame beans in their pod (175 g without their pod)
300 g tomato
250 g cucumber
50 g red salad onion
Pickled sushi-ginger to garnish

Miso ginger dressing

4 tbsp miso, white if available
2 tbsp freshly squeezed lemon juice
(or rice vinegar)
2 tbsp maple syrup
1½ tbsp chopped pickled sushi-ginger

➤➤ Place the seaweed in a bowl and pour boiling water over. Leave for approx. 10 minutes and drain. Mix the seaweed with soy sauce and pressed garlic and leave to marinate.

➤➤ Pour the frozen beans into lightly salted boiling water. Bring the water to the boil again and boil for 3-4 minutes. Taste to make sure they are 'al dente' and crisp inside. Drain and remove the beans from the pods when they are cool enough to touch.

➤➤ Cut the tomatoes into small cubes, cut the cucumber in half lengthwise, scrape off the seeds using a teaspoon and cut into small cubes. Peel the onion and cut it into tiny cubes.

➤➤ Mix the dressing and season to taste.

➤➤ To serve: Mix seaweed, vegetables and beans and drizzle the dressing on top.

! You can use many other types of beans apart from edamame beans, e.g. 150 g dried mung beans which you cook according to the recipe page 74 (mung bean salad) Read about seaweed page 217. If you buy edamame beans already podded, there is no need to boil them, just defrost them. Edamame beans are available from Asian specialist shops.

Sliced

Smoked cheese
raw salad

RAW green cabbage salad with apple, hazelnuts and berry vinegar

Green cabbage salad is excellent with spelt pancakes.

300 g green cabbage leaves
100 g hazelnuts – or walnuts
1 sweet crisp apple
100 ml concentrated blueberry-
  blackcurrant- or aronia juice
4-5 tsp berry vinegar, e.g.
  raspberry, cider or cherry
  vinegar
Salt and freshly ground pepper

❯❯ Rinse the green cabbage thoroughly in several lots of clean water so the soil drops to the bottom of the basin. Cut away the stalk and chop the green cabbage leaves finely with a sharp cook's knife.

❯❯ Chop the nuts coarsely and toast until golden in a dry, hot frying pan (avoid the small bits which burn easily), save half for garnishing.

❯❯ Remove the core from the apple and cut into small cubes.

❯❯ Mix the green cabbage thoroughly with nuts, apple, juice and berry vinegar. Season to taste with salt, pepper and extra vinegar.

❯❯ Garnish with the rest of the nuts.

! Good juices are available from health food shops.

smoked CHEESE salad

Smoked cheese gives a wonderful flavour and can be used for lots of dishes, this is a raw salad

1 bunch radishes
200 g carrots
200 g beetroot
½ tsp fennel seeds, caraway or
  cumin
100 g Greek yogurt 10% or
  natural yogurt 3.5 %
100 g *rygeost* 10% (unmatured
  smoked Danish cheese) or if
  unavailable, another smoked
  cheese or feta
1 clove garlic, pressed through a
  garlic press
Salt and freshly ground pepper

❯❯ Pinch off the top of the radishes and peel the carrots and the beetroot. Grate everything on the coarse side of the vegetable grater.

❯❯ Grind the fennel seeds, caraway or cumin in a mortar.

❯❯ Mix yogurt and smoked cheese with the spices and pressed garlic. Mix the vegetables with the smoked cheese cream (save a little for garnishing) and season to taste with salt and pepper. Garnish with the rest of the vegetables.

! Read about *rygeost* on page 217.

Japanese INSPIRED red cabbage salad

300 g red cabbage
1 (300 g) fennel
1 lemon
1 small bunch chives or fennel
  top
A little pickled sushi-ginger to
  garnish

Dressing
1 tbsp wasabi
2 tbsp soy sauce
1 tbsp clear honey

›› Remove the outermost leaves of the cabbage and cut the rest finely.

›› Cut the fennel in half through the root and cut into thin slices lengthways.

›› Peel the lemon, cut the fruit into very thin slices and cut these into halves or quarters. Cut/clip the chives or fennel top into small pieces. Chop the ginger coarsely.

›› Mix the dressing and season to taste.

›› To serve: Mix the dressing with cabbage and fennel. Decorate with lemon, chives and ginger.

! Read about the Japanese ingredients pages 216-217.

White cabbage salad with dried fruits, NUTS and tahini dressing

450 g white or pointed cabbage
10 (60 g) dried dates
4 (100 g) dried figs
70 g hazelnuts
Peel of 1 organic lemon
1 small bunch dill

Tahini dressing
3 tbsp tahini
1 clove garlic, pressed through a
  garlic press
Approx. 3 tbsp water
1 pinch cayenne pepper or more
Salt
4 tbsp freshly squeezed lemon
  juice

›› Dressing: whisk the tahini in a bowl until it is smooth. Add the pressed garlic, salt and cayenne pepper. Whisk in, a little at a time, the lemon juice and the water with the dressing – first it becomes thicker, then thin again until you have a thin cream. Season the dressing to taste: It should preferably be a little acidic.

›› Remove the outermost leaves of the cabbage and cut the rest finely.

›› Cut the dates and the figs into thin slices. Chop the nuts coarsely and toast in a dry hot frying pan until golden brown (do not include the small bits, which will burn).

›› Grate the lemon peel very finely. Chop the dill coarsely, do not use the stalks.

›› To serve: Mix the red cabbage with the dressing and serve, garnished with the dried fruits, nuts, lemon peel and dill.

! Read about tahini page 217.

Sliced

White cabbage salad
with dried fruits, nuts
and tahini dressing

Japanese inspired
red cabbage salad

Classic hummus

Middle East salad topping

Fennel tomato topping

The CREAMY salads

These salads are excellent as a sauce and to add a creamy element to your plate.

HUMMUS with variations

Traditionally hummus is served flat on a plate and drizzled with olive oil, paprika and a little chopped parsley. You use hot pita bread to scoop up the hummus on your plate. We do not recommend using tinned chickpeas here – they have an odd taste. The water from chickpeas can be used in the hummus. It does not contain toxins which certain types of bean have.

CLASSIC hummus

200 g dried chickpeas
Vegetable stock, 3 bay leaves, or
   herbs for boiling
3 tbsp tahini
1 garlic clove, peeled and
   crushed
2-3 tbsp freshly squeezed lemon
   juice
1 tsp ground cumin
Approx. 150 ml water from the
   chickpeas or water
Salt and cayenne pepper

A little olive oil and paprika and
   parsley for garnish
Pita bread for serving

Toppings
see page 88

>> Soak the chickpeas overnight in plenty of cold water, discard the water and boil for 2-3 hours in fresh water with the 'flavouring' added of your choice. The chickpeas should be completely soft. Add a little salt at the end, pour off the water and save for later.

>> Blend the peas with a hand blender or in a food processor with the other ingredients, season to taste.

>> Serve on a plate or in a bowl, and drizzle oil over, sprinkle with paprika and a little chopped parsley.

Sliced

HUMMUS toppings

Middle East salad topping

In the Middle East they eat finely sliced salads morning, midday and evening. The smaller the salad is cut the better the flavours are mixed in your mouth.

200 g sweet tomatoes
150 g cucumber
200 g red sweet pepper
1 tbsp chopped red salad onion
   or onion
Chopped parsley, mint or
   coriander for garnish

Dressing
1 tbsp freshly squeezed lemon
   juice
1 tbsp good olive oil
1 garlic clove, peeled and
   crushed
1 pinch cinnamon
½ tsp sumac (optional)
Salt and freshly ground pepper

>> Cut the tomatoes into small cubes and drain in a sieve. Cut the cucumber lengthways, remove the seeds with a teaspoon and cut it into small cubes. Remove the seeds and cut the pepper into small cubes. Mix all vegetables and onion.

>> Mix the dressing and add to the salad just before serving, season to taste.

>> Serve the salad on top of the hummus or serve on the side.

! Sumac is an aromatic, acidic red-brown powder made from the dried seeds of a fruit which grows in the wild in the Mediterranean and the Middle East. Available from well stocked grocers, it can also be used as a sprinkling on salads and in dressings as we have done here.

Fennel tomato topping

250 g fennel
250 g sweet tomatoes
½ tsp fennel seeds (optional)
1½ tbsp freshly squeezed
   lemon juice
1½ tsp clear honey
Salt and freshly ground pepper

>> Cut away any brown spots on the fennel, remove the outer leaves and wash thoroughly. Cut the rest into quarters and cut everything into thin slices with a sharp knife.

>> Cut the tomatoes into small bits, chop the fennel seeds coarsely.

>> Mix fennel, tomato and fennel seeds with lemon juice and honey and season with salt and pepper.

>> Serve as topping on the hummus or separately in a bowl.

Sliced

TURBO hummus from split peas

This hummus is made from yellow or green split peas – yes the kind you use for old fashioned pea soup and not much more. Split peas need considerably shorter cooking time than chickpeas and they do not need soaking, so long term planning is not necessary. We add exotic flavourings to the hummus – it simply tastes better than flavour enhancers such as cider vinegar, caraway seed and thyme.

250 g yellow or green split peas
600 ml vegetable stock
1 tsp cumin seeds
1½ tsp dark sesame oil
1 clove garlic, pressed through a garlic press
4 tbsp freshly squeezed lemon juice
Approx. 1 tsp salt

Topping (optional)
Radish, carrot, spring onion or finely sliced pointed cabbage
Olive oil

>> Boil the peas in water and vegetable stock. Turn the heat down low and leave the peas to cook for approx. 30 minutes until tender. Green split peas need a little longer.

>> Mash the peas in the stock left over from cooking and leave to cool.

>> Stir the cumin seeds in a dry hot frying pan until fragrant and grind in a mortar.

>> Season the hummus with cumin, sesame oil, pressed garlic, lemon juice and salt.

>> Serve with finely cut colourful vegetables on the top and a little olive oil drizzled over.

! Split peas are rather soft when they have just been cooked. But they will thicken as they cool. Don't despair therefore if the hummus does not have the right consistency while it is still warm; add a little water, if necessary if the hummus is too thick when cool.

Sliced

Imagine the enormous
energy concentrated in an
acorn! You put it into the
soil and it explodes into
an oak tree. If you bury a
sheep it simply rots.
George Bernard Shaw, writer

Celeriac cream with FRESH goat's cheese

This is a super delicious and exciting way of using celeriac. Tastes delicious with quinoa patties with beetroot page 28, potato pancakes page 44 or with oven baked potatoes and mixed salad.

½ (approx 400 g) celeriac
50 g goat's cream cheese or
  ordinary good cream cheese
Salt and freshly ground pepper

>> Peel the celeriac and cut into large cubes/chunks. Put in a saucepan, just cover with water and boil the celeriac for approx. 20 minutes under a lid, until completely tender.

>> Save a little of the cooking water and discard the rest. Blend the celeriac with the cream cheese to a smooth puree and add cooking water, if necessary, if the puree is too thick.

>> Carefully re-heat the puree in the saucepan making sure it does not boil and season to taste with salt and pepper.

! Add fresh chopped herbs just before serving such as parsley, thyme, dill, chives or cress.

Crisp cauliflower DILL cream

Serve this cream with potato pancakes page 44 and root vegetable pancakes page 42 or with oven baked potatoes and mixed salad.

200 g potatoes
300 g cauliflower including stalk
200 g raw cauliflower
1 red chilli
1 tbsp good olive oil
30 g freshly grated parmesan
1 clove garlic, pressed through
  a garlic press
2 tbsp chopped dill
¾ tsp salt

>> Peel the potatoes. Cut the potatoes and the 300 g of cauliflower with stalk into large chunks. Put into a saucepan, cover with water and boil for approx. 15 – 20 minutes until tender.

>> Discard the water and blend potatoes and cauliflower.

>> Cut the raw cauliflower into small cubes.

>> Cut the chilli in half, remove the seeds and chop finely.

>> Mix the raw cauliflower and chilli with the cauliflower cream and add the oil, parmesan and pressed garlic and dill. Add salt to taste.

Celeriac cream

Cauliflower dill cream

AUBERGINE salads

The mild

2 aubergines
1 + 1 tbsp olive oil
2 cloves garlic, pressed through
   garlic press
2 tbsp freshly squeezed lemon
   juice
Salt

Topping
1-2 tomatoes
1 handful basil leaves or broad
   leaved parsley
1 handful fresh parmesan
   shavings (optional)

≫ Remove the stalks from the aubergines. Cut each aubergine into 6 wedges. Place on a baking sheet lined with baking paper, drizzle with 1 tbsp oil and mix well with the oil.

≫ Bake the aubergines in the oven at 220C/gas 7 for 20-25 minutes, until golden brown and tender. Leave to cool a little.

≫ Blend the aubergines in a food processor or with a hand blender with pressed garlic, oil, lemon juice and salt to make a soft puree. Season to taste.

≫ Cut the tomatoes into small cubes. Chop the basil or parsley coarsely.

≫ Serve the puree in a serving dish and sprinkle with tomato cubes, basil or parsley and parmesan shavings, if using.

The wild

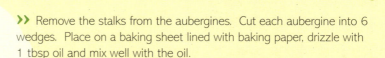

2 aubergines
1 tbsp olive oil
2 cardamom pods
1 green chilli
6 cloves garlic
½ tsp black peppercorns
1 tsp cumin seeds or caraway
   seeds
1 bunch fresh coriander
Salt

≫ Remove the stalks from the aubergines. Cut each aubergine into 6 wedges. Place on a baking sheet lined with baking paper, drizzle with 1 tbsp oil and mix well with the oil.

≫ Bake the aubergines in the oven at 220C/gas 7 for 20-25 minutes, until golden brown and tender. Leave to cool a little.

≫ Cut open the cardamom pods and remove the seeds. Cut the chilli in half and remove the seeds.

≫ Add garlic, cardamom seeds, chilli, pepper, cumin or caraway and the bunch of coriander with stalks to a food processor or mini chopper. You can also put it in a bowl and use a hand blender. Blend to a smooth uniform puree.

≫ Add the aubergines and blend. Season the aubergine salad to taste. Garnish with a little fresh coriander.

Mild aubergine salad

Classic Raita

Smoked cheese
raita

Wild aubergine
salad

RAITA

Raita is the Indians' answer to tzatziki. It has a slightly thinner consistency and is used to cool hot food (see photo page 95).

Classic Raita

½ cucumber
1 tomato or banana
500 ml natural yogurt
½ tsp cumin seeds
Salt

≫ Cut the cucumber lengthways, remove the seeds with a teaspoon and cut it into small cubes. Cut the tomato or the banana into small cubes.

≫ Toast the cumin seeds in a dry pan until fragrant. Grind lightly in a mortar.

≫ Mix the yogurt with the cumin, cucumber and tomato/banana and season with salt to taste.

! You can use all kinds of vegetables and fruits cut into small pieces in this raita. And you can season it with approx. ½ tsp finely grated fresh ginger

Smoked cheese raita

The smoked cheese gives a piquant smoked flavour to the raita. Read about smoked cheese page 217.

2 (800 g) ripe mangoes
1 large handful freshly chopped mint, parsley or coriander
1 garlic clove, peeled and crushed
150 g *rygeost* (unmatured smoked Danish cheese) or if unavailable other smoked cheese or feta
150 g Greek yogurt 10% or regular yogurt 3.5%
Salt

≫ Cut along the sides of the stone of the mango at the broadest side. Peel the mangoes with a small knife. Also peel the rest of the mango. Cut the flesh away from the stone and cut the flesh into small cubes.

≫ Save a few herbs for garnish, mix all ingredients and season the raita to taste. Leave to settle in the fridge.

≫ Garnish with the rest of the herbs.

! You can use tomatoes and cucumbers instead of mango, 500 g in total cut into small cubes. Or bananas or pineapple.

Sliced

Cucumber-radish-smoked cheese cream

A classic salad which is delicious with potato pancakes see page 44.

**Approx. 200 g *rygeost* or if
unavailable other soft cheese
such as goat's**
200 ml natural yogurt
1 cucumber
1 bunch radishes
1 bunch chives

›› Mix the smoked cheese until smooth with the yogurt a little at a time.

›› Cut the cucumber in half and slice thinly. Cut the radishes into thin slices lengthways. Save a little for garnish and mix the rest with the smoked cheese cream and season to taste with salt and pepper. Serve in a dish.

›› Sprinkle with chopped chives, cucumber and radish.

Variation on TZATZIKI

Tzatziki is traditionally made with cucumber, garlic and Greek yogurt. These are variations for your inspiration. Empty your fridge and make your own.

Basic cream:
200 ml Greek yogurt 10% fat
1-2 garlic cloves
Salt

» Mix the yogurt with garlic pressed through a garlic press. Mix in one of the following vegetables or fruit and season with salt to taste.

With beetroot

With apple

lassic with cucumber

With pointed cabbage

Fillings, choose from

- 300 g coarsely grated carrots, or beetroot
- 300 g cauliflower cut into fine small florets, small cubes or thin slices cut with a sharp knife or grated coarsely on a vegetable grater
- 100 g finely cut pointed cabbage
- 100 g finely cut baby spinach
- 1 coarsely grated cucumber, small cubes or halved, seeds scraped out and cut into ½ cm thin slices, preferably diagonally
- 300 g melon, apple, pineapple, mango, banana, strawberry or pear, cut into small cubes.

Autumn salad

Winter salad

Summer salad

Spring salad

The LIGHT salads

This is the light, crisp part of the salad buffet, or just the inspiration for your daily salad. We have made a salad for each of the four seasons but they are conceived as an inspiration for your own compositions. Mix the green lettuce leaves of your choice with fibrous vegetables such as finely cut cabbage, root vegetables or fruit and /or watery vegetables such as tomato, cucumber and radishes. Choose a dressing and topping which goes with the dish you are serving. If you are having Asian food, serve the seasonal vegetables with an Asian dressing or topping. Use the seasonal chart on page 226 for finding vegetables and fruit. See dressings and toppings page 102-103.

Mix and match the salads with dressings and toppings on the next page.

! Remember to rinse and dry the lettuce leaves well, use a salad spinner.

Spring salad

100 g baby spinach
200 g pointed cabbage cut into thin strips
1 bunch radishes, cut into slices
1 bunch spring onions, cut thinly diagonally

Summer salad

1 lettuce, little gem, frisée or romaine
200 g lightly cooked fresh green beans
½ fennel cut into paper thin slices
250 g halved cherry tomatoes

Autumn salad

1 lettuce, crisp or oak leaf
1 large carrot cut into thin sticks
1 apple cut into thin wedges
Leaves of 3 sprigs thyme
1 red salad onion cut into thin slices

Winter salad

100-150 g baby leaves or 2 little gem lettuces
200 g finely cut red cabbage
1 small onion finely chopped

Sliced

Oil-VINEGAR dressings

>> Choose the dressing, mix in all the ingredients and season to taste. Carefully mix the dressing with the salad and season to taste again.

Southern Europe
1½ tbsp olive oil
1 tbsp balsamic vinegar, wine vinegar
 or sherry vinegar
Salt and freshly ground pepper

Japanese
1 tbsp dark sesame oil
1 tbsp freshly squeezed lemon juice
50 ml soy sauce
1 tbsp pickled finely chopped sushi-ginger

South American
1 finely chopped red chilli
2-3 tbsp lime juice
1 tbsp olive oil
Salt and freshly ground pepper

Northern Europe
4 tsp cold pressed rapeseed oil
3-4 tsp cider vinegar
Salt and freshly ground pepper

Asian
1 tbsp soy sauce
1 tbsp lime juice
1 tbsp neutral tasting oil
2 tsp peeled, freshly grated ginger
1 garlic clove, peeled and finely grated

Indian
1½ tbsp lime juice
2 tbsp neutral tasting oil
1 tsp curry powder
1 garlic clove, peeled and crushed
Salt

Creamy dressings

Thousand island
150 ml sour cream
1 tbsp ketchup
½ tsp Worcester Sauce
1 garlic clove, peeled and crushed
Salt

>> Mix all the ingredients and season to taste.

Curry dressing
150 ml sour cream
1 tbsp curry powder
4 tsp freshly squeezed lemon juice
1 tsp honey
Salt

>> Mix all the ingredients and season to taste.

Herb dressing
150 ml sour cream
1 tsp finely grated organic lemon peel or
   2 tsp Dijon mustard
3 tbsp finely chopped herbs, such as
   parsley, dill, chives, basil, chervil,
   tarragon, lemon balm or mint
Salt and freshly ground pepper

>> Mix the sour cream with lemon peel, if you want the fresh flavour – otherwise Dijon mustard if you want it a little sharper. Add the herbs and season with salt and pepper to taste. Blend the dressing to make it uniformly green and to bring out the herb taste more intensely.

Granny dressing
A classic creamy dressing, where the lemon juice thickens the cream a little. Traditionally you add a little sugar, but try it without. Delicious and fresh with chives or dill. Or try a new version: 'Hippie-granny with a kick' and add 1 clove pressed garlic to taste.

100 ml whipping cream
1 tbsp freshly squeezed lemon juice
Salt and freshly ground pepper and sugar (optional)
1-2 tbsp finely chopped chives or dill (optional)
1 garlic clove, peeled and crushed (optional)

>> Mix all the ingredients and season the dressing to taste.

Toppings

>> Choose a topping and sprinkle over the salad just before serving:

- Toasted sesame seeds, pumpkin seeds, sunflower seeds or linseeds
- Toasted chopped nuts
- Freshly chopped herbs, such as watercress, cress, chives or dill, basil, tarragon, lovage etc.
- Nori sheets cut into strips or seaweed crumbled over

Sliced

SAUCES

cold and
hot sauces
and dips

The following sauces and dips
go well with pasta, potatoes,
rice, quinoa, noodles etc.

The COLD sauces

Mojo

A spicy chilli sauce which goes well with oven baked potatoes in their skin, oven baked root vegetables and polenta.

4 fresh red chillies
1 tsp ground cumin
2 cloves garlic
½ tsp salt
½ tsp paprika, smoked, if
 available
50 ml olive oil
1-2 tbsp sherry vinegar
 or other wine vinegar

>> Cut the chillies in half, remove the seeds and cut them into rough pieces. Leave to soak in a bowl of cold water for 15 minutes.

>> Pour away the water from the chillies and blend chilli with cumin, garlic, salt, paprika, olive oil and 1 tbsp sherry vinegar. Add a little water if the mixture is too thick for the blender.

>> Season with more sherry vinegar and salt to taste.

Romesco sauce with SAFFRON

This sauce goes well with pasta, potatoes, rice or quinoa accompanied by falafel page 33 or quinoa patties page 28.

2 kg red peppers
2 + 4 tbsp olive oil
2 cloves garlic
100 g almonds, walnuts or
 hazelnuts
1 large pinch saffron
Approx. 3-4 tbsp balsamic
 vinegar
Salt and freshly ground pepper

>> Cut the peppers in half, remove the seeds and place on a baking tray lined with baking paper with 2 tbsp oil. Bake in the oven at 200C/gas 6 for approx. 45 minutes, until golden brown and tender. Turn the vegetables once during cooking. Add coarsely chopped garlic for the last 5 minutes of the cooking time.

>> Place the almonds on a baking tray and put in the oven together with the peppers. Toast for approx. 10 minutes, until golden and fragrant.

>> Soak the saffron in 1 tbsp water for 5 minutes.

>> Blend the peppers and garlic to a uniform mixture with the saffron and the water from the saffron and 3 tbsp balsamic vinegar. Add the almonds last – they should be coarsely chopped.

Season to taste with salt, pepper and extra vinegar.

Romesco sauce

Mojo

Horseradish cream

Hot tomato dip

Bearnaise cream

HORSERADISH cream

Goes well with spelt pancakes page 61 and potato pancakes page 44.

300 ml sour cream
  or crème fraîche 9%
3 tbsp fresh finely grated
  horseradish
½ tsp salt

›› Mix the sour cream with horseradish and add salt to taste. Add more horseradish to the cream to taste depending on the strength of the horseradish.

Bearnaise CREAM

Goes well with baked potatoes or potato wedges.

1 shallot
6 sprigs fresh tarragon or 1 tsp
  dried
50 ml white wine
300 ml crème fraîche 18% or
  sour cream 9%
Salt and freshly ground pepper

›› Chop the shallot and 4 sprigs tarragon finely and boil with white wine in a saucepan until all the wine has evaporated. Leave the onions to cool.

›› Pick off the leaves from the remaining 2 stalks of tarragon and chop finely.

›› Mix the onions with the crème fraîche or sour cream and tarragon. Add salt and pepper to taste.

Hot tomato dip

Goes well as a dip with tortilla chips and with tortilla wraps page 65.

400 g tin chopped tomatoes
Approx. 25 g pickled jalapeno
  chillies, green or red
1 clove garlic
1 tsp sugar
½ tsp salt

›› Blend tomatoes, chillies, garlic, sugar and salt to a puree and season to taste.

! The tomato dip can also be made with 400 g fresh ripe tomatoes. Do not skin the tomatoes. Add a small tin of concentrated tomato puree to intensify the flavour and the colour.

The HOT sauces

Wild MUSHROOM sauce

This sauce goes well with pasta and polenta or just as a ragout served with bread or an omelette.

400-500 g porcini (ceps)
2 cloves garlic
2 tbsp olive oil
100 ml white wine
50 ml coarsely chopped flat leaf
  parsley
Salt and freshly ground pepper
1-2 tsp lemon juice

>> Clean the porcini and cut into 2 cm thick slices or cubes of 2 x 2 cm. Cut the garlic into half.

>> Heat the oil in a frying pan with the garlic. Fry the mushrooms in the oil at medium heat for 3-4 minutes.

>> Add white wine and leave to simmer for 5 minutes.

>> Add parsley and season with salt and pepper and lemon juice to taste. Bring the mushrooms to the boil briefly and serve immediately.

Variation: The mushrooms taste delicious whether sliced or cubed. You can also take off the cap from the porcini and fry it whole with the stalk cut into slices.

! You can use chanterelles, oyster caps, or other wild mushrooms instead of porcini.

Sauces with DRIED mushrooms

These go well with pasta, polenta and fried or boiled potatoes.

50 g mixed, dried mushrooms
100 g onions
1 tbsp olive oil
250 g fresh mushrooms
Water, if necessary
250 ml whipping cream
50 ml chopped parsley
1 tsp finely grated organic
  orange peel
Salt

>> Put the dried mushrooms in a bowl and cover with 400 ml water. Leave in a cool place for at least 2 hours.

>> Peel the onion and chop it. Fry in the oil at medium temperature for 10 minutes until clear. Stir frequently.

>> Remove the mushrooms from the water without stirring too much. Chop the mushrooms coarsely on a chopping board. Put a clean dish cloth or tea towel in a sieve and pour the mushroom water through so any sand will be removed.

>> Mix the dried mushrooms with the onions and fry for a couple of minutes. Clean the fresh mushrooms and chop them roughly. Add to the mixture and fry for 5 minutes. Add the water from the mushrooms a little at a time and leave the sauce to simmer under a lid for 30 minutes. Add a little more water to stop the mushrooms drying out.

>> Add cream and boil without a lid until the sauce has a delicious creamy consistency.

>> Add chopped parsley and season with orange peel and salt.

Wild mushroom sauce
page 109

Tomato sauce with star anise
page 113

Spinach-silverbeet sauce
page 112

Steamed polenta
page 48

Sweet pepper sauce
page 112

Grilled polenta
page 48

Sauce with dried mushrooms
page 109

SWEET pepper sauce

Goes well with polenta and boiled or sauteed potatoes, root vegetable pancakes page 42 or potato pancakes page 44.

2 red peppers
100 g shallot or 150 g ordinary
  onions
150 g carrots
2 tsp olive oil
100 ml vermouth
100 ml white wine
200 ml vegetable stock
Salt

➤➤ Remove the seeds from the peppers and cut into large cubes and cut the peeled onions and peeled carrots into small cubes.   Fry in a saucepan in the oil but do let them brown.

➤➤ Add vermouth and white wine and boil until the liquid has almost evaporated.

➤➤ Add the vegetable stock and boil under a lid until all the vegetables are tender.

➤➤ Blend to a fine and uniform puree. Add salt to taste.

! Add a little white vinegar to taste. Use white wine or vermouth or use 200 ml vegetable stock instead..

SPINACH-silver beet sauce

Goes well with mushroom-walnut pâté page 41 and with pasta, polenta and new potatoes.

500 g fresh spinach or silver
  beet leaves
1 clove garlic
2 tbsp olive oil
4 tbsp water
Chilli flakes
salt

➤➤ Rinse the spinach with the stalks thoroughly in several lots of cold water.

➤➤ Boil the spinach until tender in a saucepan with 100 ml water and 1 clove garlic cut into slices.

➤➤ Blend the spinach to a smooth puree with the olive oil. Season with salt to taste and sprinkle chilli flakes on top.

I➤➤ f you use silver beet: Cut the large green leaves off the stalks. Rinse the leaves thoroughly and boil like spinach.

➤➤ Meanwhile rinse the stalks thoroughly, use a vegetable brush to remove all soil from the cracks. Cut the stalks into 1 cm thick pieces, diagonally. Fry at once in a little oil – they turn black if left for too long – while stirring until tender.   Mix in the blended sauce.

! Add a little water or vegetable stock to the sauce and serve as a soup.

! Use frozen spinach instead of fresh.

Tomato sauce with STAR ANISE

Goes well with quinoa, tortilla wraps, potato- or root vegetable pancakes and with potatoes.

2 cloves garlic, pressed through
   garlic press
2 tsp neutral tasting oil
½ tsp smoked paprika powder
   or rose paprika
1 star anise
1 cinnamon stick
400 g tin chopped tomatoes
1 tsp dark Muscovado sugar or
   soft brown sugar
Salt

≫ Fry the garlic in a saucepan in oil with paprika, star anise and cinnamon.

≫ Add tomatoes, sugar and salt.

≫ Leave the sauce to simmer under a lid for approx. ½ hour. Season to taste.

TOMATO SAUCE à la Era Ora

The tomato sauce from Italian restaurant Era Ora in Copenhagen is the world's best because you flavour it with orange juice which both emphasizes the tomato's acidity and sweetness in a harmonious and surprisingly fresh way. The basil flavour is delicious in the sauce, while it is simmering and the parmesan, which you add at the last minute, brings a salty taste to the sauce and makes it lightly creamy. Serve with rye pappardelle page 130 or just boiled good quality pasta.

4 fresh tomatoes
1 clove garlic
3 tbsp olive oil
Juice of 1 orange
1 handful basil leaves
Salt
1 handful fresh parmesan
   shavings + a little for
   garnishing

400 g dry pasta or 500 g fresh

≫ Remove the stalk from the tomatoes with a sharp vegetable knife and cut a small cross in the skin on the opposite side. Place the tomatoes in boiling water for 5 seconds and put into a bowl of cold water. Remove the skin and cut each tomato into 6-8 wedges.

≫ Cut the garlic in half and simmer tomatoes and garlic in a saucepan at medium heat for 3 minutes. Add orange juice and coarsely chopped basil and leave the sauce to simmer for a further 3 minutes. Add salt to taste.

≫ Boil the pasta in a large saucepan in lightly salted boiling water until al dente. Drain the pasta but save a little of the water. Turn the pasta in the sauce, add the parmesan and bring the pasta carefully back to the boil for a moment. Add a little of the water from the pasta, if the sauce is too dry. It should be creamy and juicy round the pasta. Serve immediately with parmesan shavings.

Sauces

pasta and noodles
rice and grain
quinoa and potatoes

! You can cheat a little and add 500 ml vegetable stock and leave the rice to simmer under a lid for 10 minutes to begin with, instead of adding it during the cooking. Continue to stir.

In this chapter you will find several main courses for every day or for a party.

RISOTTO with asparagus and spinach

Risotto should be eaten as soon as it is cooked – the family should be ready with the forks which is the only necessary tool. Remember that the rice should be a little al dente just like pasta with a slightly crisp centre. The finished risotto should float a little on the flat plate on which it is served. Serve this spinach risotto with a couple of lemon wedges for drizzling over and the rest of the parmesan for sprinkling.

200 g onions
1 tbsp olive oil
400 ml risotto rice or ordinary pudding rice
200 ml white wine
Approx 1½ litres vegetable stock
500 g (1 bunch) green asparagus
100 g baby spinach
50 g freshly grated parmesan
1 clove garlic
Salt and freshly ground pepper
Finely grated zest of 1 organic lemon
1 lemon cut into wedges

›› Peel and chop the onions. Fry in the oil in a large saucepan until clear but not browned. Add rice and leave to fry for a couple of minutes with the onion.

›› Add white wine to the rice and keep stirring until the wine has evaporated. Continue to stir. Add 200-300 ml boiling vegetable stock and continue to stir. Leave the rice to cook at medium high temperature, stir frequently and continue to add boiling vegetable stock as the rice absorbs it. The rice should be creamy all the time and the liquid almost massaged into the rice while you stir.

›› Break off the woody ends of the asparagus. Rinse and cut them into slices of 2-3 cm. Add to the risotto when it has cooked for approx. 15 minutes.

›› Rinse the spinach and add to the risotto when the rice is almost tender but still with a slight bite. Carefully stir while the spinach wilts.

›› Season the risotto to taste: Put half the parmesan into the risotto, add finely chopped garlic, salt and pepper, ½ - 1 tsp finely grated lemon zest and extra vegetable stock, if necessary. The consistency of the perfect risotto is creamy and with a little 'sauce' between the rice. Adjust the consistency with water or vegetable stock right up until serving.

! Risotto is an Italian primi course, that is the carbohydrate rich dish between first course (antipasti) and the main course – with lots of vegetables. Primi is typically pasta, soup, polenta and risotto. Outside Italy a portion of risotto may make up the main course, followed by a salad. Forget all about full fat restaurant-risottos with lots of cream and butter, which is quite unnecessary and in large doses completely un-Italian. The rice makes the sauce deliciously creamy in itself, just helped by a little freshly grated parmesan. Hot and filling.

Rice in a BOWL with Thai salad

A super fresh and light dish with hot rice and cold, crisp vegetable topping. You can also use ordinary white rice but the brown tastes of more, is more filling and contains healthy fibre which aids digestion.

300 ml brown jasmine rice
600 ml water

Summer topping
1 cucumber
400 g cherry tomatoes
1 bunch spring onions
1 lettuce
1 bunch fresh coriander

Dressing
4 kaffir lime leaves or 2 lemon
   grass stalks
1 small red or green chilli
1 clove garlic
3 tbsp soy sauce
5 tbsp lime juice (juice of 2-3
   limes)
1 tsp cane sugar
1 tbsp neutral tasting oil

>> Measure rice out in a measuring jug. Boil in 600 ml of water according to the instructions on the packet.

>> Cut the cucumber into small cubes and the tomatoes into quarters. Cut the spring onions into thin slices. Rinse and dry the salad and cut it finely. Roughly chop the coriander.

>> Fold each kaffir lime leaf and pull off the stalk. Chop the leaves very finely. Cut the chilli in half, remove the seeds and chop it finely. Chop the garlic finely.

>> Mix the lime leaves, soy sauce, lime juice, chilli, garlic and cane sugar.

>> To serve: Mix the cucumber, tomato and spring onions with the dressing and season to taste.

>> Put the rice in 4 bowls and place the topping over the rice. Sprinkle with the chopped coriander.

Winter topping
It takes a little time to cut the vegetables finely as described, but it is worth the effort as they are easier to eat and you will have more flavours in your mouth at the same time.

400 g cauliflower
400 g carrots
1 sweet crisp apple
3 sticks celery with leaves
1 large red salad onion
1 small bunch fresh coriander
   or Thai basil

Dressing
As a summer version

>> Cut the cauliflower, both florets and stalk into cubes of approx. 1 x 1 cm. Or cut into thin slices, that looks beautiful.

>> Cut the peeled carrots into thin slices lengthways, first one way then the other to make short sticks the size of match sticks.

>> Cut the apple into the same shapes. Cut the celery into thin slices and chop the green leaves. Peel the onion and cut it into thin wedges.

>> To serve: Mix the dressing and add the vegetables and mix thoroughly.

>> Serve the topping on brown jasmine rice and sprinkle with coriander or Thai basil.

! Lemon grass: Remove any rough outer leaves, cut off the end and cut the lowest third of the grass very finely. The rest of the lemon grass can be used in a stew or soup.

! This topping also goes well with 1 ripe avocado cut into small cubes.

Both toppings are also delicious served as salads.

Winter topping

Summer topping

Quinoa with mango and MISO-ginger dressing

200 ml whole quinoa
350 ml water
Salt
2 leeks
1 ripe mango
1 cucumber

Miso ginger dressing

1½ tbsp chopped pickled
    sushi-ginger
4 tbsp miso, white or red
3 tbsp lemon juice or rice
    vinegar
2 tbsp clear honey
2 tsp dark sesame oil

>> Measure out the quinoa in a measuring jug. Rinse it in cold water in a sieve. Boil the quinoa in 350 ml water in a saucepan under a lid at low heat for 10 minutes, remove from the heat, add salt and stir.   Leave the saucepan with the lid on for 10 minutes or a little longer until all the water has been absorbed and the grain is soft and loose.

>> Remove the root and outer leaves of the leeks. Cut the leek into 1 cm thick slices diagonally, wash these in several lots of clean water. Put aside a small handful of green leek top for garnishing. Put the rest in a bowl and pour boiling water over. Leave on one side for approx. 5 minutes, until they are slightly crisp, then drain.

>> Peel the mango, cut the flesh and slice into sticks.

>> Cut the cucumber lengthways, remove the seeds with a teaspoon and cut it into small slices diagonally.

>> Mix the ingredients for the dressing and season to taste.

>> Add the hot quinoa to individual bowls and place the vegetables and fruit on top. Drizzle with the dressing and decorate with leek top.

! Read about quinoa, miso and sushi-ginger on pages 216-217.

Rice & beans

Go wild with vitamins, proteins and iron. Beans and rice is a classic combination which makes up the basic diet for a large proportion of the earth's population. The basis for this recipe was to make a dish which contained ingredients that had the maximum proteins, vitamins, minerals and healthy oils. That the dish became one of this cookbook's most successful recipes and Bille's absolute favourite luckily refutes any allegation that there is a conflict between health and pleasure. Try it! The salad is also delicious on its own, when the beans and rice are served either hot or lukewarm.

200 g white or brown dried
    beans, such as borlotti and/or
    pinto beans.
3 cloves garlic, 3-4 sprigs thyme,
    rosemary or sage or 2 tsp
    dried and vegetable stock for
    boiling
1 handful arame seaweed
200 g green cabbage or other
    cabbage
2 red peppers
3 tbsp pine kernels
400 ml brown jasmine rice or
    other rice
2 ripe avocadoes

Miso dressing
9 tbsp miso, red if available
3 tbsp maple syrup
4 tbsp apple cider vinegar
1 clove garlic, pressed through
    a garlic press
150 ml water

>> Soak the beans overnight in plenty of cold water. Discard the water and boil the beans with chopped garlic, herbs and plenty of vegetable stock as indicated on the packet. The cooking time depends on the type of bean but expect a minimum of 1 hour. The beans should be completely tender and soft.

>> Pour boiling water over the seaweed and leave for approx. 10 minutes, then drain.

>> Chop the green cabbage finely, discard the coarse stalks.

>> Remove the seeds and cut the peppers into small cubes.

>> Mix miso, maple syrup, apple cider vinegar, pressed garlic and water, season to taste and add the seaweed, the pepper and the hot beans.

>> Toast the pine kernels in a dry, hot pan until golden. Leave the nuts to cool on a plate.

>> Cook the rice as indicated on the packet and serve hot or warm with the beans.

>> To serve: Cut the avocado into small cubes or slices: Put rice into individual bowls and place the beans and vegetables in the miso dressing on top. Sprinkle with toasted pine kernels and avocado cubes

! Use 400 g tinned beans if you are short of time. Rinse in water. It is o.k. that they are not hot.

! Use pumpkin seeds, sesame seeds, linseed or sunflower seeds instead of pine nuts.

! Use honey instead of maple syrup.

Winning LASAGNE with leeks and gorgonzola

Lasagne is really the name of the shape of the pasta, i.e pasta sheets and not the name of a dish. Normally you think of lasagne as an oven-baked dish. But boiled lasagne sheets put together with two delicious sauces just before serving is different and elegant. The freshly cooked lasagne sheets are unbelievably delicious and the experience is a light and fresh dish in contrast to the heavy, oven-baked lasagne. It demands a little extra attention, so make it when there are only two for dinner – a real winner. Serve a large bowl of salad to eat after the lasagne, with a couple of good cheeses.

For 2 people

Tomato sauce
100 g onions
25 g sun-dried tomatoes
1 tbsp olive oil
400 g plum or cherry tomatoes
1 clove garlic
2 sprigs fresh sage
Salt and freshly ground pepper

Gorgonzola sauce
100 ml whipping cream
75 g gorgonzola
Freshly ground pepper

Approx. 125 g fresh lasagne
  sheets

>> The tomato sauce: Peel and chop the onion finely and cut the sun-dried tomatoes into broad strips. Fry the onion and sun-dried tomatoes in the olive oil at medium heat for 5 minutes and stir often so the onions do not colour.

>> Cut the plum or cherry tomatoes in halves and add to the pan with the coarsely chopped garlic and sage. Leave the sauce to simmer for 10 minutes. Add salt and pepper to taste.

>> Gorgonzola sauce: Boil the cream in a saucepan and leave to cook for 4 minutes until it thickens a little. Add the gorgonzola in small bits and mix with the cream. After you have added the gorgonzola the sauce burns easily so keep an eye on it.

>> Lasagne: Bring a large saucepan of lightly salted water to the boil.

>> Cut the lasagne into pieces of approx. 12 cm at the wide end. If the lasagne is in pieces in the packet you just halve them.

>> When the sauces are ready, the table laid, the wine opened and everyone is ready to eat, finish cooking the lasagne. Place the pieces in the boiling water one by one so they do not stick together. Cook the lasagne for the number of minutes indicated on the packet or until it has finished cooking to al dente.

>> Remove the lasagne from the water using a perforated skimmer. Leave to drain on a tea towel.

>> Place a piece of lasagne on each plate enough to fold it a little. Add a couple of tbsp tomato sauce and a couple of tbsp gorgonzola sauce to the lasagne. Place another piece of lasagne on top of the tomato sauce and add another portion of tomato sauce on top of the lasagne. Place the last lasagne sheets on the plate and the gorgonzola sauce on top of each lasagne. Grate pepper over the gorgonzola sauce and serve immediately.

! You can use good quality dry lasagne instead of fresh lasagne.

! You can use wild mushroom sauce page 109 or spinach sauce page 112 instead of tomato sauce.

! A little less fat: Use 100 ml cream 9% with milk and 1 tsp cornflour in a saucepan instead of whipping cream. Bring to the boil while continuing to stir and add the gorgonzola.

Spinach lasagne

Serve this spinach lasagne with lemon wedges and chilli sauce or chilli flakes and a large bowl of salad.

2½ tbsp plain white flour
500 ml milk
500 g frozen spinach leaves
Salt and freshly ground pepper
1 pinch ground nutmeg
1 tsp finely grated organic
   lemon peel
200 g fresh lasagne
100 g coarsely grated medium
   mature cheese

>> Mix the flour with a little milk in a saucepan until smooth. Add the rest of the milk and bring to the boil while continuing to stir.

>> Add the frozen spinach to the sauce and cook and continue to stir until all the spinach is defrosted.

>> Mix salt, pepper, nutmeg and lemon peel to taste with the spinach sauce.

>> Place a little spinach sauce at the bottom of an oven proof dish of approx. 20 x 25 cm. Place a layer of lasagne on top and approx. a quarter of the spinach sauce on top. Sprinkle with a little cheese. Put another layer of lasagne on top, then spinach etc. Save a little spinach sauce and some of the cheese for topping.

>> Cover with foil. Bake the lasagne in the oven at 200C/gas 6 for 30 minutes. Remove the foil and bake the lasagne until golden on top. Also prick it to see whether the pasta is tender.

Root vegetable lasagne

This lasagne is super simple and only requires minimum vegetable cutting work. The béchamel sauce is speedy and low in fat and only needs to be brought to the boil to stop it curdling. It is almost as quick as opening a jar of ready-made sauce, but it tastes much better and contains no unnecessary or unknown ingredients. Serve with a seasonal crisp salad with an acidic dressing.

Grilled vegetables
500 g celeriac
500 g carrots
1 tbsp rapeseed – or olive oil
Salt and freshly ground pepper

Béchamel sauce
500 ml milk
5 tsp cornflour
Salt and freshly ground pepper

Tomato sauce
2 x 400 g tins chopped
   tomatoes
2 cloves garlic, pressed through
   garlic press
1 tsp ground cumin
1 tsp dried thyme
¼ tsp cayenne pepper
1 tsp salt

10-12 lasagne sheets
125 g grated cheese, such as
   cheddar

Bread tin of approx. 1½ litres

>> Turn on the oven at 220C/gas 7. Peel the root vegetables and cut into approx. 1½ x 1½ cm cubes. Add the oil to a plastic bag and shake the vegetables in this. Pour onto a baking tray lined with baking paper in one layer, sprinkle with salt and pepper and bake in the oven for approx. 15-20 minutes until golden brown. Meanwhile make the two sauces. Turn down the temperature to 200C/gas 6 when the vegetables are ready.

>> Mix milk and cornflour in a saucepan and bring to the boil while stirring. Add salt and pepper to taste.

>> Mix the tomatoes with pressed garlic, cumin, thyme, cayenne pepper and salt. Mix the baked vegetables with the tomatoes.

>> Add a little tomato-vegetable mixture to the base of the baking tin. Place a layer of lasagne sheets on top and a layer of the tomato-vegetable mixture on this. If necessary, break the lasagne sheets if they are too long, they should not overlap. They are easy to break by placing them over the edge of a table and then break with a quick and firm touch. Pour béchamel sauce on to the tomato vegetable mixture and sprinkle with a little cheese. Place another layer of lasagne sheets, tomato vegetable mixture, béchamel sauce, cheese, etc. Finish with a little tomato-vegetable mixture, béchamel sauce and cheese on top.

>> Cover with foil and bake the lasagne in the oven for 30 minutes. Remove the foil and bake the lasagne for a further 15 minutes. Also prick it to see whether the pasta is tender.

! Use a mild or strong cheese depending on how much you want the lasagne to taste of cheese. Or try a hard, white goat's cheese. Different cheeses will give a different character to your lasagne.

! You could use other root vegetables instead of a quarter of the celeriac and carrots, parsnip, Hamburg parsley, beetroot, turnip or kohlrabi.

Rye pappardelle

Home-made pasta. Rye is rarely used in Italy but it tastes really fantastic in pasta and gives a coarser consistency and a more filling pasta. The rye flour makes it difficult to roll the dough very thinly and the pasta will therefore be wonderfully rustic which is charming, since it does not affect the flavour.   Does the recipe seem long and complicated? Maybe, but it is really super simple, and in the meantime you will get lots of good tips on how to make pasta.   Serve with tomato sauce à la Era Ora page 113, spinach sauce page 112 or sauce of dried mushrooms page 109 and a bowl of crisp salad.

Pasta dough

250 g durum flour (grana duro)
   or plain white flour
75 g coarse rye flour
4 eggs, lightly beaten

>> Pasta: Mix the flours together in a medium sized bowl. Make a well in the centre of the flour and pour the beaten eggs into it.

>> Using the tips of your fingers, mix the eggs with the flour, incorporating a little at a time, until everything is combined. Turn the dough out onto a board. Then you can start to knead the dough with your hands.

>> Knead the dough well for 3-4 minutes and only add a little extra flour to the board at a time. Wash your hands in between with cold water, so the dough does not stick too much. The dough should be really firm so the finger mark stays in the dough when pressed. Wrap the dough in cling film and leave in the fridge for 30 minutes to 2 hours.

>> Roll by hand or use a pasta machine and cut into approx. 2 cm broad strips.

>> Bring a large saucepan of lightly salted water to the boil.

>> Make the sauce.

>> The pasta: Boil the pasta to al dente in boiling water. Drain the pasta but save a little of the water. Turn the pasta in the sauce, add the parmesan and bring the pasta carefully back to the boil for a little. Add a little of the water, if the sauce is too dry. It should be creamy and juicy round the pasta. Serve immediately with grated parmesan.

! Roll the dough by hand

Divide the dough in two. Press one piece of dough flat and roll it out using a rolling pin. Make sure that there is flour on the table under the dough and on top of the dough which should be easy to slip off the table while rolling.

>> Roll the dough as thinly as you are at all able to.

>> Roll the dough at both sides towards the middle. Cut the pasta into the width you want.

>> Bring the knife under the middle of the roll and pull it up so the pasta rolls out. Make sure to roll the dough immediately.

>> Cut the pasta if necessary so it is not too long, 30 cm is the maximum.

>> Make small bunches of the pasta on the table. Curl it up a little and sprinkle flour between the pasta to stop it sticking.

>> Roll out the other piece of dough in the same way.

! Boiling pasta

Pasta should be cooked in a large saucepan of boiling lightly salted water with ample room so it does not stick together. If you use a large saucepan of water it will also get back to boiling point more quickly after adding the pasta. It is important that the pasta is boiling all the time. Use approx. 2 tbsp salt for 5 litres of water. The water needs to be salty to give flavour to the pasta. The idea is that the pasta should have flavour especially when the sauces are very simple. The water should boil all the time. Otherwise the pasta becomes sticky on the surface and it will be difficult to cook it properly.

Check the pasta frequently while it is cooking until it has the right consistency, al dente (which means on the tooth), i.e. when it is tender but with a little bite in the middle. Break a small piece of the pasta and bite it. It is better that it is a little too hard when you take it out, you should be able to bring the sauce to the boil again without overcooking the pasta.

Drain the pasta but save a little of the water.

Rye pappardelle with
tomato sauce à
la Era Ora, see page 113

Potato-spinach MASALA (See photo page 63)

Serve this dish with chickpea pancakes page 62 and raita page 96 or just rice and maybe a salad.

1 kg potatoes
200 g red salad onion
7 whole cardamoms
¾ tbsp cumin seeds
¾ tbsp coriander seeds
¾ tbsp garam masala or curry powder
1 tbsp neutral tasting oil
50 ml water
2 cloves garlic, pressed in a garlic press
Cayenne pepper to taste
450 g frozen spinach leaves
Salt

>> Scrub or peel the potatoes. Cut into cubes of approx. 2 x 2 x 1 cm. Peel the onion and cut it into approx. 1 x 1 cm cubes.

>> Cut the cardamoms with a knife and remove the seeds. Toast the cardamom seeds, cumin and coriander in a dry frying pan until fragrant, while shaking the pan all the time. Add the spice mixture to a mortar or coffee grinder and chop finely or coarsely.

>> Fry the onions in the oil for a couple of minutes, add the spices and garam masala, continue to fry for a further ½ minute while stirring. Add potatoes and fry and stir for 1 minute, add water, pressed garlic, salt and cayenne pepper.

>> Leave to simmer under a lid for approx. 15 minutes until the potatoes are cooked. Add the spinach which does not need to be defrosted, continue cooking under a lid until the spinach is warmed through and season to taste.

! You can use ground spices instead of whole and just toast them in the oil with the onions.

! You can use fresh spinach instead of the frozen; if you use fresh spinach you will need a little less.

! Read about garam masala and Nigella seeds pages 217-218.

Quinoa-pilau (See photo page 147)

Serve hot as accompaniment to Indian dishes, such as dahl page 146, curry page 149 and potato-spinach-masala above.

10 whole cardamoms
2 star anise
10 whole cloves
200 g onions
2 tsp neutral tasting oil
400 ml whole quinoa
700 ml water
100 ml raisins
50 g almonds or other nuts (optional)
½ tsp salt

>> Start buy getting all the spices ready. Cut the cardamoms open with a knife.

>> Peel the onion and cut it into cubes. Fry in the oil in a saucepan for a couple of minutes and stir until the onions are soft but not brown.

>> Rinse the quinoa in a sieve and add to the saucepan with the spices. Fry for a couple of minutes and stir without the quinoa colouring. Add water and raisins cut into smaller pieces and leave the pilau to simmer under a lid for 10 minutes. Remove the saucepan from the heat, mix in a little salt and leave on one side for 10 minutes under a lid.

>> If using, chop the almonds roughly and toast in a dry, hot pan.

>> To serve: Arrange the pilau in a serving dish and sprinkle with the almonds.

Hot & Filling

133

Creamy potatoes with turnip

Creamy potatoes made with whipping cream taste better, but it is a high fat dish which is more suited to party food than everyday food. Creamy potatoes can also be made with cream 9% which improves the dish in terms of health, but it looks a little different and the sauce is not quite as creamy round the potatoes. You can also choose a compromise and use 100 ml whipping cream mixed with 100 ml milk. Serve a large portion of salad or raw vegetables and good bread.

800 g potatoes
300 g turnip, Chinese radish or Jerusalem artichokes
1 tsp salt
Freshly ground pepper
1 pinch ground nutmeg
350 ml whipping cream or cream 9%
1 clove garlic, pressed through a garlic press

>> Peel the potatoes and the turnips. The turnips can also be scrubbed, if they are good quality. Cut into thin slices and place in alternate layers in an ovenproof dish. The bigger the dish the less cooking time is required. Sprinkle with salt, pepper and nutmeg between the layers. Place them as roof tiles if you have the time and inclination otherwise just put them all in together.

>> Whisk the cream with the pressed garlic and pour the mixture over potatoes and turnips.

>> Bake the potatoes in the oven at 180C/gas 4 for 30-50 minutes, until the potatoes are tender when pricked with the sharp end of a small knife.

! The turnip is in season from June-October but is usually available all autumn as, like all root vegetables, it keeps well. You can use Chinese radish or Jerusalem artichokes instead of turnip. The Jerusalem artichokes are best if just scrubbed with a vegetable brush but you can also peel them.

! Use root vegetables instead of half of the potatoes -
celeriac, carrot, parsnip, Hamburg parsley, kohlrabi or
sweet potato.   Other vegetables such as fennel, celery,
green cabbage, spinach, cauliflower, Brussels sprouts or
squash also work in this recipe.

Burning love remix

The vegetarian's burning love: Mashed potato with courgette topping. Mashed potato can become an everyday-party food if you embellish it a little. Be inspired by our topping suggestions or use what you have in the fridge. Serve with a crisp salad.

Mash
1½ kg potatoes
Water for boiling
Salt and freshly ground pepper

Topping
2 courgettes
1 tbsp olive oil
1 clove garlic
1 organic lemon
Salt and freshly ground pepper
4 tbsp capers
1 bunch parsley

>> Peel the potatoes. Boil in unsalted water, just covering the potatoes, until they are tender.

>> Save 100-200 ml of the water and discard the rest.

>> Mash the potatoes with a potato masher, a good large whisk or an electric whisk.

>> Add a little of the cooking water to give it a soft and light consistency. Add salt and pepper to taste.

>> Cut the courgettes across lengthways and cut into slices of ½ cm.

>> Fry the courgette in the oil in a frying pan at medium temperature and stir all the time until soft but not brown.

>> Add finely chopped garlic, 2 tsp finely grated lemon peel and 2-3 tbsp lemon juice. Add salt and pepper to taste.

>> Place the courgette over the mashed potatoes and sprinkle with capers and chopped parsley.

Other suggestions for topping
- Mushroom sauce, see page 109.
- Good olive oil, lemon oil, truffle oil or other oils.
- Smoked paprika or sun-dried tomatoes.
- Bits of smoked cheese, goes well with a mash of new potatoes.
- Feta and chopped olives.
- Pesto.

Hot & Filling

A nation's standing and moral
progress can be measured on how
it treats its animals – but it is
something far bigger which makes
us vegetarians.

Mahatma Gandhi, politician

Sweet potatoes with soy and ginger

These sweet potatoes taste delicious with buckwheat noodles, with crisp vegetables and sesame mayo page 72, mung bean salad with pineapple and chilli lime dressing page 74 or quinoa patties page 28

500 g sweet potatoes
75 ml soy sauce
2 tbsp finely grated fresh ginger
2 cloves garlic
Lime wedges to serve (optional)

>> Peel the sweet potatoes and cut into cubes of 1 ½ x 1 ½ cm. Place in a small ovenproof dish lined with baking paper.

>> Mix soy sauce with ginger and finely chopped garlic and pour the mixture over the potatoes.

>> Bake the potatoes in the oven for approx. 30 minutes at 180C/gas 4 until al dente.

! You can use squash or carrots instead of sweet potatoes.

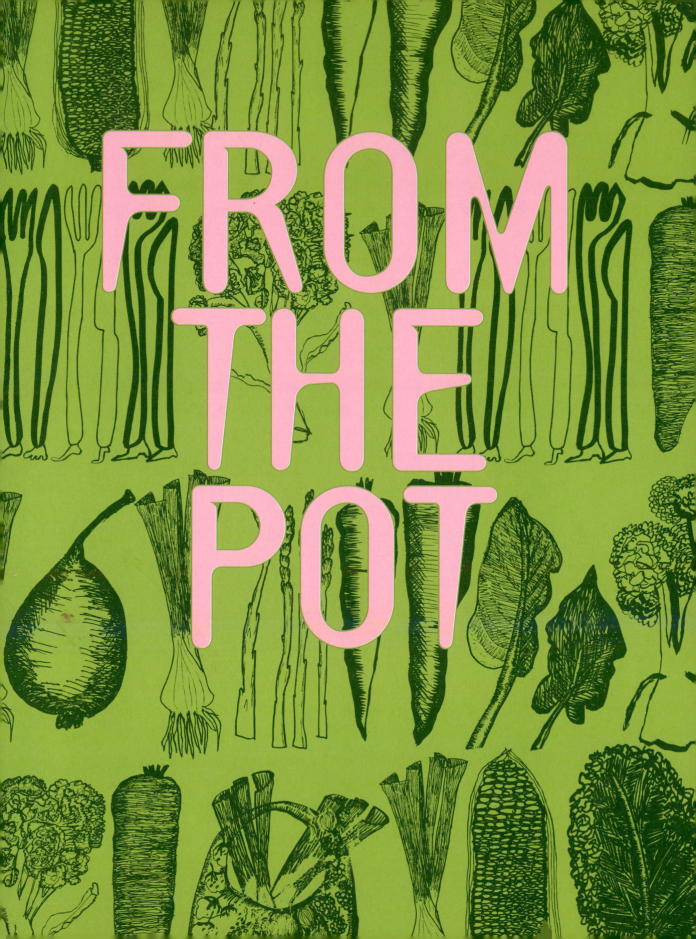

cooked and good from the pot

! You can make the pesto with basil or parsley
instead of lovage. You can also use almonds,
hazel- or walnuts instead of pine nuts.

This is a chapter with wonderful hot and filling ragouts, wok dishes, dahl, curries and hot pots which will warm you and your family during the cold months.

Bean RAGOUT with lovage pesto

The black eye bean is a fine little bean, maybe one of the tastiest of all the dried beans. It should be cooked for a long time to be tender but will rarely be overcooked and mushy. Serve this ragout with a large bowl of crisp salad.

300 g black eye beans (600 g boiled)
5 cloves garlic, 3-4 sprigs rosemary, sage or lovage or 2 tsp dried and vegetable stock for boiling

Ragout
750 g potatoes
¾ (approx 500 g) celeriac
400 ml water
Salt and freshly ground pepper

Lovage pesto
1 bunch lovage
1 clove garlic
4 tbsp olive oil
25 g freshly grated parmesan
50 g pine nuts

>> Soak the beans overnight in a bowl with plenty of water. Discard the water and cook the beans under a lid with whole garlic cloves, sprigs of fresh or dried herbs and plenty of vegetable stock until tender. This will take a minimum of 1 hour. Add boiling water during the cooking if the vegetable stock evaporates. Drain the beans when cooked.

>> Peel the potatoes and celeriac and cut into cubes of approx. 1½ x 1½ cm.

>> Put the potato and celeriac cubes in a saucepan with 400 ml water and bring to the boil. Turn down the heat and leave to simmer under a lid for approx. 15 minutes until the potatoes are tender without being over cooked. Stir now and then and add a little extra water to avoid it going dry.

>> Pesto: Rinse the lovage and pick the leaves off the stalks. Chop or grind the lovage leaves with garlic, olive oil, parmesan and pine nuts to a coarse paste.

>> To serve: Mix potatoes and celeriac with beans and pesto and season with salt and pepper to taste.

! You can use mojo page 106 or romesco sauce page 106 instead of pesto for the ragout.

Umbrian lentils

A rustic Italian lentil ragout. Red lentils are not suitable for this dish as they will boil to a mush and they do not have the delicious al dente quality which is necessary in this dish. Serve as it is in soup bowls with a little bread and a salad.

300 g fennel
350 g onions
300 g carrots
300 g celery
4 cloves garlic
1 tbsp olive oil
400 g Puy lentils, beluga lentils or small Italian lentils, picked over and washed
2 litres vegetable stock
4 sprigs sage or rosemary
The zest of 1 organic lemon
1 small bunch parsley
Salt

Topping
Chilli flakes, (optional)
A little extra good quality olive oil

›› Clean the fennel, onions, carrots and celery and cut into cubes. Fry all the vegetables and coarsely chopped garlic in the oil in a saucepan. Leave to simmer at medium temperature for 5 minutes so they develop fragrance and flavour.

›› Add lentils, vegetable stock and herbs. Cut the peel off the lemon with a potato peeler, without taking off too much of the white and add the peel to the saucepan.

›› Cook the dish under a lid until the lentils are a little tender, adding more water/vegetable stock if the lentils become too dry or flavour is missing. Add salt to taste.

›› To serve: Add chopped parsley. Serve the lentils in soup bowls with bread and a sprinkling of chilli flakes and a little olive oil.

! The lentils should be very tender and thicken the dish. If the lentils you have are not properly cooked through, you can remove some of the cooked ones, blend them and then add them to the dish.

! Use 'beluga lentils' which are very beautiful black lentils. They are unfortunately not so black when they are cooked, but have the right shape and consistency for this dish. Small Italian lentils are available from Italian delis.

Tina's dahl

This is not the world's easiest dahl, but it tastes fantastically delicious. First bring out the spices and prepare them, then the rest is easy. We have omitted onions to make it easier and because lots of garlic tastes wonderful. The dish should be hot! Serve with rice or quinoa-pilau page 133, and a seasonal salad, page 101.

5 whole cardamoms
1 tsp anise seed or fennel seed
¾ tsp cloves
2 tsp coriander seeds
2 tsp cumin seeds
Chilli flakes (or other type of chilli) of your choice
7 cloves garlic
2 tbsp finely grated fresh ginger
1 tbsp neutral tasting oil
2 tbsp curry powder and/or garam masala
5 bay leaves
½ cinnamon stick
400 g red or yellow or brown lentils
Approx. 800 ml vegetable stock
2 x 400 g tins chopped tomatoes
Salt (optional)

›› First bring out all the spices. Cut the cardamoms open with a knife and remove the seeds.

›› Toast the cardamom seeds, anise, cloves, coriander and cumin in a heavy saucepan at high heat until fragrant and they are popping, stir all the time. Grind the spices in a mortar or electric coffee grinder.

›› Chop the garlic and ginger and fry in oil while stirring for a few minutes, add curry powder and garam masala and fry for a further few minutes. Add the freshly ground spices and fry briefly, then add bay leaves, cinnamon, lentils, vegetable stock and tomatoes.

›› Leave the dish to simmer for 1 hour when the lentils will be cooked, but it may be cooked for longer if you have the time. Stir frequently. Add salt to taste.

! You can make a turbo dahl by using ground spices. Toast the curry powder and /or garam masala in the oil with the garlic, ginger and one or two of your favourite spices. Use less of the strongest tasting. Strong spices are clover, anise, cardamom – see quantities above for inspiration. Tip: You can add vegetables to the dish towards the end of the cooking time, such as frozen spinach or vegetables cut into small pieces.

Tina's dahl

Quinoa-pilau
see page 133

! Add cooked chickpeas
if you want a more filling
dish.

Sunday CURRY

Empty the fridge and make a curry of what you have. We call it Sunday curry because you can use what you have in the fridge and store cupboard already. We have made a version with summer vegetables, but you can use whatever you have.
Serve with rice or quinoa.

4 tbsp curry powder and/or garam masala
2 tsp turmeric if you are using garam masala
1 tsp ground cardamom
½ tsp ground cloves
Cayenne pepper to taste
400 g onions
4 cloves garlic
2 tbsp neutral tasting oil
2 large tins (280 g) concentrated tomato puree
900 ml vegetable stock
4 eggs (optional)
1¼ kg vegetables, e.g. a mixture of cauliflower, fennel, pepper, green beans and spinach
500 ml natural yogurt or other similar dairy product
Salt (optional)
Lime wedges to garnish (optional)

>> First bring out all the spices.

>> Peel and chop the onions. Fry in the oil in a saucepan for a couple of minutes. Add finely chopped/pressed garlic and spices and continue to cook, stir all the time. Add tomato puree, vegetable stock and leave the sauce to simmer under a lid for approx. 30 minutes while stirring frequently.

>> Boil the eggs until hard boiled for 8-9 minutes.

>> Cut the vegetables into small bits including the stalk of the cauliflower. Add the vegetables to the sauce and cook for a further approx. 10 minutes until crisp, stir frequently. Add the yogurt and season the curry to taste. The yogurt may boil. Add salt to taste.

>> Serve with rice and hard boiled eggs cut into half and lime wedges (optional).

! Leave out the yogurt and replace some of the vegetable stock with coconut milk, a small tin or light coconut milk.

! A winter version with winter vegetables could be root vegetables, cabbage, frozen peas and potatoes. The cooking time should be adjusted to the size of the vegetables.

Vegewok with SOY-madagascar peppercorn sauce

Cooking with a wok is a wonderful quick cooking method and that is precisely the whole idea behind the wok. In parts of Asia where fuel is scarce, it is useful to have a very thin metal saucepan which will become red hot very quickly. The food to be cooked in a wok is cut into small bits so it will be cooked very quickly. You stir constantly during cooking to avoid the food burning. The food cut into small bits is also easier to eat, when you are using chop sticks or a spoon. The original woks are made of thin metal and most suitable for gas, but a large saucepan or large frying pan which can be heated up to high temperatures can be used instead. Choose seasonal vegetables and sauces of your choice. Serve with rice or noodles.

Soy-madagascar peppercorn sauce
4 tbsp soy sauce
2 tsp syrup from preserved ginger
2 pieces of ginger preserve, finely chopped
2 tsp Madagascar peppercorns or to taste
1 garlic clove, peeled and crushed
4 tbsp freshly squeezed lime juice

Summer vegetables
500 g asparagus
1 bunch spring onions
2 small or 1 large courgette
150 g sugar snap peas
250 g cherry tomatoes
1 tbsp neutral tasting rapeseed oil

>> Mix the ingredients for the sauce.

>> Clean the vegetables. Break off the woody ends of the asparagus and cut into 3-4 pieces diagonally. Cut the spring onions in the same way. Cut the courgettes into slices of 3-4 cm. Sugar peas and cherry tomatoes can remain whole.

>> Heat the oil in the wok and add the vegetables which need the longest cooking time: Courgette, asparagus and spring onions. Fry and continue to stir the vegetables to avoid them burning. After 1-2 minutes add sugar snaps and cherry tomatoes. Fry for a further 1-2 minutes and add the sauce, fry it up a little and add more soy sauce, ginger syrup or lime juice to taste.

Try the same sauce with winter vegetables:
500 g leeks
400 g carrots
250 g mushrooms
150 g bean sprouts

>> Clean the vegetables. Slice the leeks thinly diagonally. Cut the carrots lengthways before slicing, this gives them a beautiful shape. Slice the mushrooms.

>> Fry the vegetables at high heat for 4-5 minutes and stir all the time. Add bean sprouts and soy-madagascar peppercorn sauce. Bring to the boil and season with more soy sauce, ginger syrup or lime juice to taste.

! See also Vegewok with Thai coconut sauce page 154.

! If you miss protein, you can use silken tofu as topping, as seen in the photo, or towards the end of the cooking time add the firm type of tofu cut into cubes.

! If the quantity of vegetables is too big for the wok, pot or pan, cook one half portion at a time.

Summer vegetables

Tofu in CHINESE sweet-sour sauce

Do not be put off by the length of the list of ingredients. Most of the ingredients are quite ordinary basic ones which most well stocked kitchens will have already. The vegetables could be just what you have or can easily get hold of, since all sorts of vegetables taste delicious in this dish, even cucumber and radishes. A really good 'empty the fridge and freezer' dish. With this meal you can eat huge quantities of vegetables. You can easily use up to 1¾ kg vegetables including pineapple. Variety in the vegetables is important, so make sure to include both some fibrous root vegetables and cabbage types and some of the watery ones: Tomatoes, bean sprouts, radishes, peppers, sugar snaps etc. Always add a few from the onion family: Onions, leeks or spring onions. Fry the coarse vegetables in the oil before adding the sauce. Only add the watery ones when the sauce is at boiling point. You can use all kinds of tofu for this dish, as long as it is the firm variety. Serve with boiled jasmine rice and extra chilli, chilli sauce or sambal oelek.

200 g carrots or other root vegetables
300 g leeks
200 g celeriac
300 g pointed, white or savoy cabbage
200 g tomatoes
300 g pineapple
½ cucumber
1 bunch radishes
1 tbsp neutral tasting oil or peanut oil
½ tsp ground anise or 3 whole star anise
2 cloves garlic
1 tbsp finely grated fresh ginger
600 ml vegetable stock
1 small tin (70 g) concentrated tomato puree
100 ml vinegar, rice vinegar, if available
2 tbsp soy sauce
2 tbsp sugar
2 tbsp cornflour
100 g frozen peas
Salt
2 tsp dark sesame oil if available
Chilli sauce, chilli flakes or sambal oelek
Approx. 300 g firm tofu, or more
1 handful fresh coriander

≫ Wash and peel all the vegetables.

≫ Cut carrots and leeks diagonally into ½ cm slices. Cut the celeriac into ½ x ½ cm sticks. Cut the cabbage into 2 cm strips, approx. 6 cm long.

≫ Cut the tomatoes into wedges and the pineapple into pieces of approx. 2 x 2 cm, cut the cucumber lengthways and cut into slices. Leave the radishes whole. Save all these vegetables for later use.

≫ Heat the oil in a large saucepan. Fry carrots, leeks, celeriac and cabbage in the oil at high heat and stir all the time so the vegetables do not burn.

≫ Add ground anise or beans from star anise, which have been lightly beaten with the side of a kitchen knife. Add also finely grated garlic and ginger. Add the vegetable stock.

≫ Mix tomato puree, vinegar, soy sauce, sugar and cornflour in a bowl until the cornflour has dissolved. Add the mixture to the vegetables and bring to the boil while stirring.

≫ Add tomatoes, pineapple, cucumber, radishes and peas and season with salt and sesame oil, which will give the authentic Chinese flavour and fragrance, chilli sauce, chilli flakes or sambal oelek if you want a hot sauce.

≫ Cut the tofu into 4 slices or large cubes and place on a dish. Pour sauce and vegetables over the tofu and sprinkle with fresh coriander.

From the Pot

Escabeche

Escabeche is normally made with fish but this version is a Spanish vegetable ragout which is served with rice or good bread or as part of a tapas selection. Saffron and smoked paprika will give a surprisingly spicy flavour.

200 g onions
200 g carrots
2 red and 1 yellow pepper
500 g ripe tomatoes
1 tbsp olive oil
2 garlic cloves, peeled and
   crushed
1 tsp paprika, smoked, if
   available
2 bay leaves
¼ tsp saffron
Salt
4 tbsp freshly squeezed lemon
   juice
2-3 tbsp wine- or sherry vinegar
1 small bunch parsley

>> Peel the onions and the carrots, remove stalks and seeds from the peppers. Cut the peppers and onions into thick slices and the carrots into thin slices.

>> Cut the tomatoes into wedges.

>> Heat the oil in the pan and fry the peppers, onions and carrots at medium heat for 5 minutes. Stir frequently so the vegetables become tender without browning.

>> Add tomatoes, pressed garlic, paprika, bay leaves, saffron and salt and fry for a further 5 minutes.

>> Add lemon juice and wine vinegar, bring to the boil for a minute and sprinkle with chopped parsley.

>> Serve the escabeche hot or lukewarm with boiled rice, quinoa or good bread.

Vegewok with Thai coconut sauce

½ deseeded chilli
100 g shallots
1 clove garlic
1 lemon grass
1 tbsp finely grated fresh ginger
1 tbsp neutral tasting oil
1-2 tsp Thai curry paste of
   your choice
1 tin coconut milk, light if
   available
1 tsp sugar
Salt
Freshly squeezed lime juice to
   taste
1 portion sliced summer- or
   winter vegetables
   See page 150

Topping
Chopped fresh coriander

>> Chop the chilli, shallots and garlic finely. Also chop the lower part of two thirds of the lemon grass. Heat the oil in the wok. Fry chilli, shallots, garlic, lemon grass and ginger for a few minutes in the oil stirring all the time. Add curry paste and fry a little more.

>> Add coconut milk, sugar and salt and cook for a few minutes.

>> With summer vegetables: Add asparagus, spring onions and courgette and cook for 2 minutes. Add sugar snaps and tomatoes and cook for 1-2 minutes. Season with lime juice, salt and sugar. Garnish with coriander.

>> With winter vegetables: Add leeks, carrots and mushrooms, fry for 4-5 minutes until tender, but al dente. Add bean sprouts, bring the sauce to the boil and season with lime juice, salt and sugar. Garnish with coriander.

From the Pot

Escabeche

Tex mex hot pot

This is a vegetarian spicy chilli sin carne.   Serve with bread, quinoa, rice or polenta, see page 48.

200 g dried kidney beans
3 bay leaves, celery top and
   vegetable stock for boiling
300 g celery
300 g peppers
300 g frozen sweetcorn

Sauce
200 g onions
4 cloves garlic
50 g almonds
1 tbsp neutral tasting oil
4 tbsp sesame seeds
1 tsp ground cloves
2 tsp ground cinnamon
3 star anise
1 tbsp lightly ground caraway
   seeds or cumin
Approx. 1 cayenne pepper or
   chilli powder
2 x 400 g tins chopped tomatoes
Approx. 300 ml lager beer,
   Mexican if available
Approx. 1 tbsp muscovado sugar
   or other sugar
40 g dark chocolate
Salt

Serve with
Tortilla chips if available

>> Soak the beans overnight in plenty of cold water. Discard the water and boil with bay leaves, celery top and plenty of vegetable stock. The beans should simmer under a lid for a couple of hours until soft and tender. Drain and discard bay leaves and celery top.

>> Sauce: Peel the onions and cut into cubes. Chop the garlic finely or press through a garlic press. Chop the almonds roughly. Fry the onion in oil in a saucepan for a few minutes over a medium heat.

>> Add garlic, almonds, sesame seeds and spices and fry for a few more minutes while stirring all the time.

>> Add chopped tomatoes, beer, sugar, chocolate and salt. Leave to simmer under a lid for ½-1 hour, stir frequently during cooking.

>> Clean and cut the celery finely and cut the pepper into smaller pieces. Add to the sauce with the boiled beans and sweetcorn. Bring to the boil and leave to simmer for approx. 5 minutes, season to taste. Serve with polenta, quinoa, rice or bread and crisp tortilla chips if available.

Animals are my friends ....
And I do not eat my friends.
George Bernard Shaw, writer

! If you are using 2 tins of beans
instead of the dried ones you can
make the dish in under 1 hour.

Chilli sin carne

Polenta

filling
soups with
lots of
vegetables

Serve the soups in this chapter as a complete meal with bread or as a first course in smaller portions.

Turbo sour-hot WHOLEGRAIN noodle soup

This soup tastes delicious with almost all kinds of vegetables. Make sure to include root vegetables and at least one kind of cabbage. Always add either leek or spring onions. The leeks should be cooked with the rest of the ingredients, but if you use spring onions, only add them at the last minute. Onions and peppers do not work so well in the soup unless they are fried first.

1 ½ kg vegetables

Should be included in the soup from the start:
Leeks cut into rings
Carrot, celeriac, parsnip or
   Hamburg parsley cut into small
   cubes, pointed cabbage, Savoy
   cabbage, white cabbage or
   green cabbage in thin strips
Cauliflower or broccoli in small
   florets
Mushrooms in slices
Fresh or frozen spinach

Should only be added at the last minute:
Beansprouts
Tomatoes cut into small cubes
Frozen peas or finely cut sugar
   snaps
Spring onions cut into thin rings

2 litres vegetable stock
250 g wholegrain noodles or
   wholegrain rice noodles
50 ml soy sauce
2 tbsp sweet chilli sauce
2 cloves garlic
3 tbsp lime- or lemon juice
1 tbsp dark sesame oil
Chopped fresh coriander, if available

›› Clean the vegetables and cut as described for the individual vegetables. Spinach may be added whole or added as frozen.

›› Bring the vegetable stock to the boil. Add the vegetables to be included from the start. Bring to the boil, add the noodles and leave to cook for the number of minutes indicated on the packet of noodles.

›› Add the vegetables to include at the last minute. Bring the soup back to the boil and season to taste with soy sauce, sweet chilli sauce, finely chopped garlic, lime- or lemon juice and sesame oil. Serve immediately and sprinkle with fresh coriander.

Wet

160

A vegetarian is a person who only eats accompaniments.
Gerald Lieberman, writer

Miso soup with PEARL barley

2 litres vegetable stock
300 ml (240 g pearl barley)
500 g mushrooms
200 g carrots
500 g broccoli or 1.25 kg
   vegetables of your choice
1 large handful (15 g) arame
   or wakame seaweed
6 tbsp miso, red if available
4 half limes for serving

Topping
3 tbsp sesame seeds
4 x ½ tsp wasabi (optional)
A little finely chopped spring
   onion or chives

>> Bring the vegetable stock to the boil in a saucepan, add pearl barley and cook under a lid until almost tender, approx. 20-30 minutes (check the cooking time for the pearl barley on the packet).

>> Wash and cut the mushrooms, carrots and broccoli finely.

>> Toast the sesame seeds in a dry, hot pan and stir all the time until fragrant and they 'pop' lightly.

>> Add the vegetables to the stock with the seaweed and cook for approx. 5 minutes.

>> Turn off the heat and whisk the miso into the soup.

>> Serve in soup bowls topped with sesame seeds and spring onions and wasabi on the side to season to taste. Lime wedges to garnish.

! Miso should not be boiling. Some misos are easier to stir directly into the soup than others. If you want to be quite sure of a uniform consistency, stir in a small bowl with a little of the hot soup before adding to the soup.

! You can use noodles instead of pearl barley. Traditionally udon noodles (thick white plain flour noodles) are used in miso soup, but you can use other types, such as the healthier buckwheat noodles or wholegrain noodles. The noodles are cooked until almost tender directly in the soup and the vegetables are added at last. It takes much less time compared to the pearl barley.

Wet

Borscht

Serve the soup with wholemeal bread.

100 g onions
5 cloves garlic
400 g root vegetables, celeriac, carrot, parsnip or Hamburg parsley
500 g beetroot
200 g pointed, white or red cabbage
1 tbsp neutral tasting oil
1 tsp caraway seeds or cumin seeds
2 tsp fennel seeds
3 bay leaves
1 pinch cayenne pepper or paprika
Approx 1.5 litres vegetable stock
Approx. 2 tbsp sugar
Approx. 3 tbsp wine vinegar
Salt

Topping
Sour cream

>> Peel and chop the onions and garlic. Peel and coarsely grate the root vegetables including the beetroot on a vegetable grater. Cut the cabbage finely.

>> Fry the onions and garlic in oil in a saucepan for a few minutes, add the other vegetables and fry for a further few minutes.

>> Grind the caraway or cumin and fennel seeds in a mortar. Mix caraway, fennel seeds, bay leaves and cayenne pepper or paprika with the vegetables and add vegetable stock and sugar. Leave the soup to simmer under a lid for 45 minutes until the vegetables are tender.

>> Add vinegar and season to taste with extra sugar, vinegar or salt. The soup should have a clear sweet & sour taste.

>> Serve the soup with sour cream on top and with some good bread.

CORN soup

This is a really rustic soup inspired by Italian vegetable soup with spelt. The soup can be made from any type of grain: Wholewheat grain, pearl rye, pearl spelt, pearl barley, cracked barley, parboiled spelt … even oats will give a delicious version of the soup, which will make it a little thicker. Use what you have, or explore the health food shop shelves or ethnic greengrocers and discover new, fun grain types for the soup: Green wheat or lightly smoked ingredients, maybe? The fresh tomatoes, garlic, parsley and a couple of drops of lemon juice will add freshness to the soup. Serve with coarse bread.

400 g celeriac
300 g carrots
3 leeks
25 g sun-dried tomatoes
1 tbsp olive oil
250g green cabbage
100 ml grain of your choice
Approx 1.5 litres vegetable stock
3 fresh tomatoes
2 cloves garlic
1 small bunch parsley
Salt and freshly ground pepper
1-2 tbsp freshly squeezed lemon
 juice

>> Peel and wash the root vegetables and the leeks. Cut the carrots and the celeriac into small cubes and the leeks into rings.

>> Cut the sun-dried tomatoes into small cubes.

>> Heat the oil in a saucepan and fry the vegetables with the tomatoes.

>> Wash the green cabbage thoroughly and cut the rough end of the stalk. Cut the rest in approx. 1 cm strips.

>> Mix green cabbage and grain with the vegetables in the saucepan and add the vegetable stock. Bring the soup to the boil, turn down the heat and leave to simmer for 20 minutes or until the grains are tender (grains vary a lot) with the lid aslant.

>> Cut the fresh tomatoes into small cubes, chop the garlic finely, chop the parsley and add to the soup at the last minute. Bring back to the boil and season to taste with salt, pepper and a little lemon juice.

>> Serve the soup piping hot with good bread.

! You can use parsnip and /or Hamburg parsley instead of some of the celeriac and carrots.

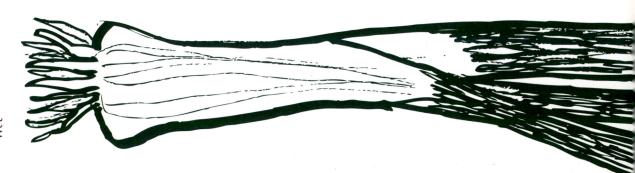

Wet

BEAN soup with pasta

This is the classic version of bean soup with pasta from the Veneto area in Northern Italy. Maybe bean soup with pasta sounds a little heavy, but the soup is surprisingly elegant and the broad pasta rolls easily around the tongue.

250 g pinto beans
3 cloves garlic
200 g onions
200 g carrots
200 g celery
1 tbsp olive oil
1 large tin (140 g) concentrated tomato puree
1 tsp cayenne pepper
2 sprigs rosemary
2 sprigs sage
Approx. 1.25 litres vegetable stock
Salt
150 g pappardelle (broad pasta strips)

Extra seasoning
- 3 tbsp olive oil
- 2 sprigs rosemary
- 2 sprigs sage
- 2 cloves garlic

>> Soak the beans overnight in plenty of cold water. Discard the water used for soaking.

>> Peel the garlic and onions and chop. Peel the carrots, clean the celery and cut into small cubes. Lightly fry the onion and garlic (pressed through a garlic press) in the oil in a saucepan for 5 minutes. Add beans, tomato puree and cayenne pepper, 2 sprigs rosemary and 2 sprigs sage, stir a little and add vegetable stock. Leave the soup to simmer for 1 ½ hours.

>> Set aside 400 ml of the vegetable- and bean filling and blend the rest of the soup until you have a fine and uniform consistency. Add the vegetables and season with salt.

>> Break the pasta into smaller bits and boil in a pot with lightly salted water. Add the cooked pasta to the soup.

>> Extra seasoning: Heat 3 tbsp oil with coarsely chopped rosemary, sage and garlic in a saucepan for 4 minutes. Strain the oil into the soup and stir.

>> Serve the soup piping hot and eat with spoon and fork.

An intellect of my
calibre cannot get its
nutrition from cows.
George Bernard Shaw,
writer

! If you cannot get hold of
pappardelle, you can use
fettuccine or pasta shells.

Creamy vegetable SOUP with herbs

Serve this soup with bread.

2 leeks
500 g cauliflower or broccoli
300 g celeriac
400 g carrots
1 squash
2 cloves garlic
200 g potatoes
2 tbsp olive oil
Approx. 1.5 litres vegetable
   stock
3 sprigs fresh thyme
2-4 chopped herbs, e.g. fresh
   mint, flat leaf or curly mint (not
   Asian), parsley and/or basil
Salt and freshly ground pepper

Topping
Chilli flakes, (optional)
A little extra good quality olive
   oil

>> Cut the leeks into slices of ½ cm. Cut the cauliflower into small florets and the stalk into small cubes. Peel the celeriac and the carrots. Cut celeriac, squash and carrots into small cubes. Cut the garlic into thin slices. Peel the potatoes and cut into halves.

>> Fry all the vegetables in the oil in a saucepan over a medium heat. Stir often and make sure that the vegetables do not brown. Leave to wilt and give off fragrance.

>> Add the vegetable stock and thyme. Leave the soup to simmer with the lid slightly aslant for 20-30 minutes, until the potatoes are tender.

>> Remove the potatoes from the saucepan along with 300 ml soup and blend. Put the blended soup back into the pot.

>> Add the chopped herbs and season with salt and pepper to taste.

>> Serve with good bread and drizzle each bowl with a little good quality olive oil and chilli flakes.

Indian PEA soup

Indian inspired pea soup.

400 g onions
2 tbsp neutral tasting oil
2 cloves garlic
2 tbsp curry powder
2 tsp ground cumin
1 large pinch ground cloves
4 bay leaves
Approx. 1.5 litres vegetable stock
200 g yellow split peas
400 g carrots
Juice of 1 lime
Salt and cayenne pepper

Topping

20 g coconut flakes or
  desiccated coconut
1 ripe mango, 1 apple or
  chopped dried apricots
Fresh coriander or mint
  (optional)

>> Peel and chop the onions. Fry in the oil until clear, add finely chopped garlic and spices and fry for a few minutes, stirring all the time.

>> Add the vegetable stock and the yellow split peas. Leave the soup to simmer under a lid for 1 hour until the peas are soft and tender.

>> Topping: Toast the coconut flakes or the desiccated coconut in a frying pan or in a little saucepan, stirring all the time until light brown. Remove from the heat immediately. Peel the mango and cut the flesh into thin slices or small cubes. Cut the apple in the same way.

>> Remove the bay leaves from the peas and blend the soup with a hand blender.

>> Peel the carrots and grate them coarsely on a vegetable grater. Add the carrots to the soup and cook for a few minutes, add a little water, more lime juice and season with salt and cayenne pepper.

>> To serve: Garnish with herbs, coconut flakes and fruit.

Wet

173

burgers
sandwiches
packed lunches

Vegetables help nature to grow
Pressure on the environment from meat production is on average 10 times greater than from vegetable production.

In this chapter we throw away the cutlery and give you ideas for super burgers and lots of suggestions for the green packed lunch.

Falafel burgers with tahini DRESSING

1 portion falafel mixture, see page 33
1 portion tahini dressing, see page 84
1 romaine lettuce
1 red salad onion
1-2 carrots
½ fresh green chilli
4 coarse burger buns, see page 186

>> On a chopping board using the falafel mixture make 4 flat burgers 8 cm in diameter. Use a knife or metal palette knife to loosen the burgers from the chopping board, and move them to the frying pan. Fry in oil in a non stick frying pan at medium temperature for approx. 5 minutes each side, until firm and golden brown.

>> Rinse the lettuce leaves and dry. Cut into smaller pieces. Peel and cut the salad onion into thin rings. Peel the carrots and cut into strips with the peeler. Cut the chilli, remove seeds and slice thinly or cut into cubes.

>> Cut the bun in half. Place burger, vegetables and dressing in layers. Or serve everything in bowls so everyone can help themselves at the table.

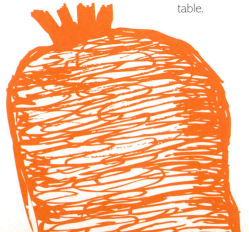

Quinoa BURGER with guacamole

Quinoa burgers fried as large burgers make an excellent burger meal. Use the recipe page 28 and make 4 burgers. Use the left over mixture for quinoa patties for the packed lunch.

1 portion quinoa mixture, see
  page 28
2 tomatoes
1-2 beetroots
1 large red salad onion
4 tbsp pickled jalapenos
4 coarse burger buns, see page
  186

Guacamole

2 ripe avocadoes
1 tbsp freshly squeezed lemon
  or lime juice
1 garlic clove, peeled and
  crushed
Salt

>> Fry the burgers.

>> Cut the tomatoes into slices. Peel the beetroots and cut into strips using the peeler. Peel and slice the onion.

>> Guacamole: Mash the avocadoes with a fork and mix with the lemon- or lime juice and garlic. Add salt to taste.

>> Cut the buns in half. Place burger, vegetables, jalapenos and guaca-mole in layers. Or serve in bowls so everyone can help themselves to build the burgers at the table.

! The burgers can also be made using the mushroom-nut recipe, page 41.

VEGE-PACKED LUNCH IDEAS
There are lots of ways of making a healthy and delicious vegetarian packed lunch.

! Use leftovers. Make large portions and use the leftovers cold for packed lunches. Suitable recipes are marked with

FILLINGS for rye bread, wholemeal bread and buns

>> Hummus page 87 and Aubergine salad page 94 are excellent spreads. Put the toppings in a small box or bag separately, or bring sliced/grated vegetables as accompaniment.

>> Avocado slices with lemon juice, sliced tomato and fresh herbs or thin onion rings and salt.

>> Ajvar (pureed pepper relish available in jars), mayo, boiled potato, sliced avocado and sliced eggs, salt and pepper make delicious spreads.

>> Sliced potato, strips of red pepper, thin onion rings and olives.

>> Sliced potato, thin onion rings, good quality mayo and a sprinkling of smoked paprika.

>> Egg salad using eggs, avocado, garlic, lemon, curry powder and salt.

>> Egg salad using mustard, boiled potatoes, onions and cornichons, pickled cucumbers or capers.

>> Scrambled eggs with sliced tomato and thin onion rings.

>> Peanut butter with sliced vegetables and salad.

>> Vege BLT: Smoked cheese as the spread, sliced tomatoes and lettuce leaves, salt and pepper.

>> Cheese spreads: Cream cheese, goat's cream cheese or smoked cheese with herbs, olives, sliced tomatoes, strips of peppers, jalapenos or cress.

>> Hard cheeses: Comté, Gruyère, Manchego, Pecorino, Cheddar — and honey, onion rings, sliced tomato, cucumber, radishes or peppers.

Sprinklings wih extra flavour

Cress, fresh herbs, grated horseradish or a sprinkling of smoked paprika.

Spread & Packed

181

BAKED GOODS & PUDDINGS

breads

puddings

muesli

This chapter covers easy and healthy recipes for home-made breads, puddings and other delicacies for breakfasts.

Wholegrain BREAD

This is the bread for those of you who do not like having your fingers in dough. The dough is mixed and poured directly into the tin, where it is left to rise. The bread will keep fresh for several days and is also delicious toasted, when it is too dry to eat fresh.   It will need to rise for 2-3 hours depending on the room temperature. Because of the slow development of the yeast and using yogurt and durum wheat, this bread develops a stronger flavour and is much juicier compared to the ordinary quickly raised plain white flour bread.   Store the bread in a plastic bag.

Makes 1 loaf

¼ packet (approx. 12 g fresh
   yeast)
350 ml cold water
100 ml natural yogurt
1½ tsp salt
1 tsp honey
50 g sunflower seeds
175 g wholemeal or coarse
   spelt flour
150 g coarse durum flour
   (grano duro)
250 g plain white flour
1 tbsp butter or oil for greasing
   the tin

>> Dissolve the yeast in the water in a large bowl; mix yogurt, salt, honey and sunflower seeds.

>> Add wholemeal-or spelt flour, durum flour and plain white flour a little at a time and mix the dough in a machine or by hand using a spoon to form a sticky dough.

>> Brush a bread tin with melted butter or oil. Pour the dough into the tin. Use a scraper or spoon dipped in a little water to smooth the surface.

>> Cover with cling film and leave to rise until double in size at normal room temperature, this will take 2-3 hours depending on the temperature of the room.

>> Bake in the oven at 200C/gas 6 for approx. 30 minutes.

>> Remove from the tin and leave to cool on a baking tray.

! You can speed up the rising time by leaving the bread in a warm place and/or use lukewarm water instead of cold water.

Cold risen BURGER buns

These buns are delicious for all kinds of sandwiches. Cold risen buns should rise overnight in the fridge. The dough is super quick to make. Just remember to prepare it the night before, and you will also have fresh buns for breakfast.

Makes 10

¼ packet (approx. 12 g) fresh
  yeast
500 ml cold water
2 tsp salt
1 tbsp rapeseed oil
1 tbsp honey
200 g coarse spelt flour or
  wholemeal flour
200 g durum flour, grano duro or
  plain white flour
200 g plain white flour

>> The night before: Dissolve the yeast in the water in a large bowl. Mix salt, rapeseed oil and honey with a spoon. Add spelt flour- or wholemeal flour, durum flour and plain white flour and mix to a thick and sticky dough.

>> Cover the bowl with cling film and leave in the fridge overnight.

>> The next day: Using two spoons shape the dough into 10 buns or dip your hands in cold water and shape the dough with your hands. Place directly on baking trays lined with baking paper.

>> Leave the buns to rise approx. 30 minutes and bake in the oven at 200C/gas 6 for 15 minutes..

RYE bread

This is an old fashioned rye bread but is still quick to make, since you bake it on the same day as you mix it. It is slightly sour with lots of texture.

Makes 1 large rye bread

1 glass sour dough (available
  from health food shops)
1 litre lukewarm water
375 g cracked rye
1 tbsp salt
375 g coarse rye flour
500 g plain white flour
1 tbsp rapeseed oil

>> Mix the sour dough with water and cracked rye in a large bowl. Add salt, rye flour and plain white flour and mix it all thoroughly.

>> Set aside 200 ml sour dough from the mixture, put it in a plastic box with an airtight lid and place it in the fridge for the next time you want to make bread. It will keep for two-three weeks.

>> Put the dough into a 1.5 litre bread tin greased with oil.

>> Leave the dough to rise at room temperature for 8 hours until it has risen one third.

>> Bake the bread in the oven at 180C/gas 4 for 1 hour, or when an oven thermometer shows 96 degrees.

>> Remove from the oven, take the bread out of the tin and leave it to cool on a cooling tray.

! Leave the bread to cool completely on a cooling tray, if you want a crisp crust. If you want a softer crust which is easier to cut, you can put the bread in a plastic bag or cover it with a clean tea towel while it is still warm.

Variation: All kinds of kernels and seeds are delicious in the bread, e.g. pumpkin seeds, linseeds, sunflower seeds and sesame seeds. Use 100-200 g of one or several different kinds.

Cold risen burger bun page 186

Wholemeal bread

Rye bread page 186

Cold risen burger bun page 186

IRON muesli

Sprinkle the muesli over your favourite sour milk product and add lots of seasonal fresh fruit or berries. Raisins or other dried fruit are also delicious, e.g. apricots, figs or dates cut into small cubes.

Makes 15 portions

2 tbsp dark Muscovado sugar
2 tsp cold pressed rapeseed oil
1 tbsp water
500 ml coarse oats
2 tbsp linseed
100 ml pumpkin seeds

›› Mix muscovado sugar, oil and water in a bowl. Measure the other ingredients. Smooth out lumps in the sugar.

›› Mix oats, linseeds, and pumpkin seeds thoroughly with the oil and sugar mixture until evenly mixed.

›› Spread the muesli onto a baking tray lined with baking paper and bake in the oven at 120C/gas ½ for 30 minutes.

›› Leave the muesli to cool on the baking tray and store in an airtight container.

A vegetarian is an individual who does not eat anything that can produce children.
David Brenner, comedian

QUINOA porridge with honey toasted pumpkin seeds and lightly whipped cream

This porridge is also delicious served for brunch. Quinoa tastes wonderful and is healthy. The whipped cream may not be so healthy but it does give a lift to the flavour. Every now and then we should just have a party.

Makes 4 large or 6-8 small portions

100 ml (50 g) pumpkin seeds
1 tbsp honey
100 ml whipping cream
400 ml quinoa flakes
900 ml-1 litre water
A pinch of salt
6-8 tbsp jam or fruit compote of
   your choice

>> Toast the pumpkin seeds in a dry hot pan until they pop and are lightly brown. Add honey, remove the pan from the heat and stir. Spread the seeds over baking paper and leave to cool a little, in the fridge, if you like, which will make them very crisp. Break into smaller pieces.

>> Whip the cream until it is lightly foamy.

>> Add the quinoa flakes to a saucepan with water and cook at medium heat while continuing to stir all the time for approx. 10 minutes until you have a soft and smooth porridge.

>> Season with salt and serve hot in individual bowls, garnished with jam, seeds and whipped cream. You can also serve the cream on the side, as it quickly melts.

! You can also use whole quinoa for porridge. For 6 people you will need 300 ml quinoa and 1.1 litres water and cook it for approx. 25 minutes. Otherwise follow the recipe above.

! You can make the porridge just before serving or make it beforehand and gently heat it up while stirring all the time, adding a little more water, as necessary.

SWEET THINGS

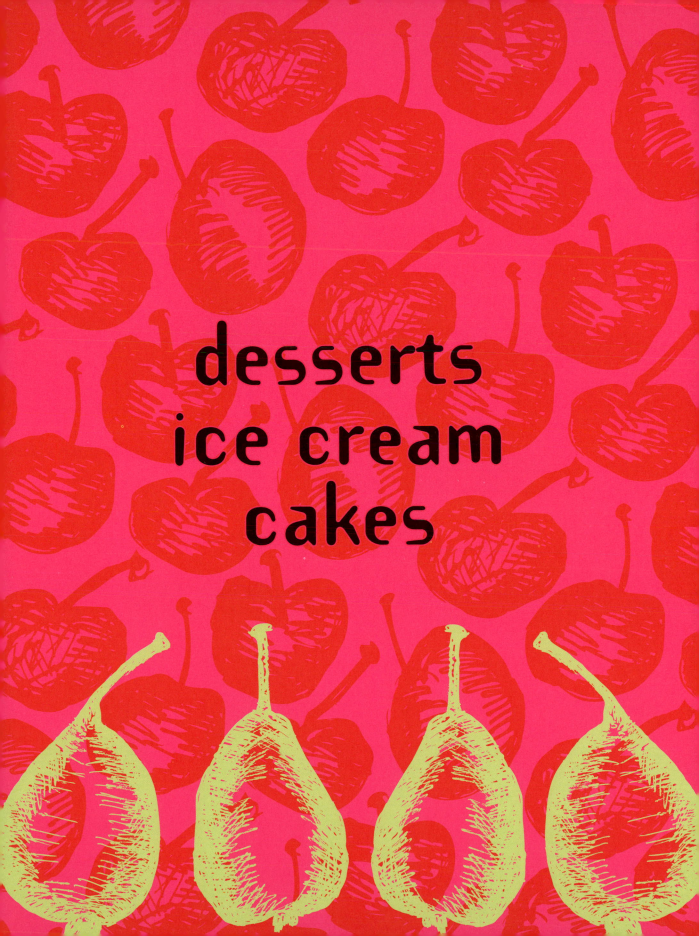

desserts
ice cream
cakes

Milk chocolate-ginger

Miso chocolate

In this chapter you will find sweet things which are either vegan, a little bit healthy such as miso or just the perfect finish to a good meal.

CHOCOLATE TRUFFLES

Serve these chocolate truffles with coffee or espresso.

Miso chocolate TRUFFLES

Miso gives an interesting, very slightly salty flavour which also goes well with the chocolate.

Makes approx. 30

200 g good quality dark chocolate
150 ml whipping cream
1 tbsp butter
2 tbsp miso, red if available

Garnish

Grated peel of 1 organic orange, chopped unsalted pistachio nuts.

>> Chop the chocolate coarsely. Gently heat the cream with the butter in a saucepan. Add the chocolate and whip it smooth. Remove from the heat, add the miso and whip until the mixture is uniform.

>> Pour into a tin, a bowl or a dish – the flatter the dish, the quicker it sets. Place the truffle mixture in the fridge or freezer for 1-4 hours until firm.

>> Make small or larger truffles with a teaspoon and roll into balls with your hands.

>> Roll the truffles in the garnish and place in the fridge until ready to serve. Serve with coffee. Mmmmmmmmmmmm.

! You can use many other kinds of nuts, e.g. almonds or hazelnuts.

Milk chocolate ginger TRUFFLES

Makes approx. 30

50 g butter
100 ml whipping cream
200 g milk chocolate
1 tbsp finely grated fresh ginger

Garnish

50 g grated white, milk or dark chocolate

>> Gently heat the butter and cream in a saucepan until simmering point.

>> Remove from the heat, add chopped chocolate and ginger. Stir until the chocolate has melted. Pour into a tin, a bowl or a dish – the flatter the dish, the quicker it sets. Leave to cool in the fridge.

>> Take a small amount of the truffle and roll it between your hands to form a bun with a diameter of approx. £1 coin.

>> Grate white, milk or dark chocolate with a potato peeler or use a vegetable grater. Roll the truffles in the grated chocolate and place in a plastic or metal box. Store in the fridge.

! The truffles can also be rolled in cocoa or toasted, finely chopped almonds instead of grated chocolate.

THE COLD SHOCK

Turbo berry sorbet

For 6 people

300 g frozen berries, e.g.
   raspberries, strawberries,
   forest berries, blueberries or
   a mixture
100 g icing sugar
1 organic lemon
100 ml water

Garnish

Fresh berries or fruit cut into
   small bits and/or whipped
   cream

» Put the frozen berries in a food processor with the icing sugar, finely grated lemon peel – and juice – and the water. Blend immediately until the mixture has a uniform consistency.

» Pour into a small square 600 ml tin and place in the freezer. After 2-3 hours it is ready to cut and can be turned out onto a plate and sliced.

» Instead of putting the sorbet in a tin you can serve it almost immediately as soft ice. Since it melts quickly it may be easier if you use a plastic bag. Pour the sorbet directly from the blender into a bag, tie a knot in the bag and place it in the freezer for 30-60 minutes. Cut a hole in the corner of the bag and squeeze the sorbet out into individual dishes.

» Decorate with fresh berries, fruit or whipped cream.

Tropical fruit coconut ice cream

Serves 8-10

1 large (approx. 700 g) ripe
   pineapple
3 ripe bananas
1 small tin (165 ml) coconut
   milk
200 ml sugar
Juice of 2 limes

Garnish

1 handful coconut flakes
4 passion fruits
Fresh pineapple and/or banana
   in small bits

» Cut the peel off the pineapple and cut out the centre. Cut 500 g pineapple into large chunks. Save the rest of the pineapple for decoration. Peel the bananas and cut into pieces. Also save a little of the bananas for garnishing. Put the fruit in a plastic bag and place in the freezer until the fruit is completely frozen.

» Place the frozen fruit in a food processor. Add coconut milk, sugar and lime juice. Blend to make a soft fruit ice cream.

» Put immediately into a square 1 litre tin and place in the freezer. After 2-3 hours it is ready to cut and can be turned onto a dish and sliced.

» Instead of putting the ice cream in a tin it can be served immediately as soft ice. Since it melts quickly it may be easier if you put it in a plastic bag. Pour the ice cream directly from the blender into a bag, tie a knot on the bag and place it in the freezer for 30-60 minutes. Cut a hole in the corner of the bag and squeeze the ice cream into individual dishes.

» Garnish: Toast the coconut flakes in a dry, hot pan until golden. Remove from the heat immediately. Cut the passion fruit in half, scrape out the flesh with a spoon and mix well. Pour the passion fruit over the ice cream and decorate with coconut flakes and small pieces of fresh pineapple and banana.

Turbo berry sorbet

Tropical fruit
coconut ice cream

! Some supermarkets sell frozen tropical fruit in
cubes. You can use 800 g of these instead of
freezing fresh fruit.

Pancakes with BEER and vanilla

This is the vegans' favourite pancake. When the linseeds are blended with the other ingredients they act as a binding agent, just like egg. Serve with marmalade, sugar, icing sugar or jam.

Makes 6 medium pancakes

150 ml rice milk, natural flavour
½ tsp baking powder
Seeds of ½ vanilla pod
30 g oats
50 g plain white flour
1 tbsp linseed
1 pinch salt
100 ml beer
2 tsp sugar
½ tsp grated organic orange peel
Neutral tasting oil (such as rapeseed oil) or coconut oil for frying

➤➤ Place all the ingredients except for the oil in a bowl or blender. Blend for 1 minute.

➤➤ Heat the oil in a small frying pan. Pour the batter into the pan and cover the pan. Use 50 ml of the mixture for each pancake.

➤➤ The pancake should be brown and crisp at the edge before turning it over and finish cooking it on the other side.

! You can leave out 50 ml rice milk and then make small, slightly thicker pancakes with the mixture. This makes approx. 10. You can use rice milk instead of beer.

! Use 100 g berries for the fruit mixture, this will make it juicier and fresher. Use frozen berries if necessary.

! Use Armagnac, rum, sherry or wine instead of cognac.

Fruit CRUMBLE

This crumble tastes delicious baked with either butter or in the vegan version with coconut oil.

Serves 4-6

50 g grated white, milk or dark
  chocolate
50 g hazelnuts
100 g oats
Seeds of ½ vanilla pod
50 light or dark muscovado
  sugar or cane sugar
125 g cold butter or 60 g
  coconut oil
600 g apples, plums or pears
  and/or berries
2-3 tbsp cognac (optional)

Serve with

Whipped cream, crème fraîche,
  sour cream or vanilla ice cream

>> Chop the chocolate and nuts coarsely.

>> Put the oats, vanilla seeds and muscovado sugar in a bowl. Cut the butter into smaller bits – if you are using coconut oil scrape it out into small bits and mix it with the other ingredients in the bowl. Crumble it all between your fingers to a uniform crumbly mixture. Do not knead too much or the dough will stick together. Quickly mix in the chocolate and the nuts.

>> Cut the plums, apples or pears without peel, seeds and stones into large cubes or small narrow wedges. Put the fruit in an ovenproof dish of approx. 24 cm diameter or 20 x 20 cm in a layer to a height of approx. 3 cm.

>> Pour over the alcohol and then the crumble topping over the fruit.

>> Bake in the oven at 180C/gas 4 for approx. 25 minutes until crumble topping is golden brown and the fruit cooked through and tender.

! You can prepare the crumble and leave it unbaked in the fridge until ready to cook.

MOUSSES
without gelatine and thereby free of pig's ears! Read about agar agar on page 217.

Mango mousse

2 mango fruits (400 g fruit)
100 ml orange juice, 'freshly
   squeezed' from a bottle, if
   necessary
100 ml water
100 g sugar
½ tsp agar agar

Garnish
Mint leaves or fresh mango
   pieces

>> Peel the mango. Cut the fruit from the stone and cut into big chunks. Blend the mango flesh with the orange juice to make a fine puree.

>> Boil water, sugar and agar agar powder in a saucepan and leave to simmer for 2-3 minutes. Blend the warm sugar mixture with the mango puree.

>> Add the puree immediately to small individual serving bowls and put in the fridge. The mousse is ready approx. 30 minutes later.

Strawberry mousse

Almond milk is the cream for vegans.

500 g strawberries
150 ml rice milk
100 ml water
100 g sugar
Seeds of ½ vanilla pod
½ tsp agar agar powder

Almond milk
50 g almonds
100 ml cold water
1 tsp icing sugar, if necessary

Garnish
Fresh strawberries in small pieces

>> Clean the strawberries and hull them. Blend the strawberries with the rice milk to make a fine puree.

>> Boil water, sugar, vanilla seeds and agar agar powder in a saucepan and leave to simmer for 2-3 minutes.

>> Blend the warm sugar mixture with the strawberry puree.

>> Add the puree immediately to small individual serving bowls and put in the fridge. The mousse is ready after approx. 30 minutes.

>> Almond milk: Blend the almonds finely with the water. Drain the almond milk and add more icing sugar, if necessary.

>> Serve the strawberry mousse with the almond milk and fresh strawberries cut into small pieces.

! You can use 400 g frozen strawberries instead of fresh ones. Defrost completely before blending.

Almond mousse

100 g almonds
300 ml soy milk or rice milk
100 ml water
1 tsp agar agar powder
50 g sugar
Seeds of ½ vanilla pod

Garnish
Fresh berries, cooked berries
   or fruit

>> Place the almonds in a saucepan and cover with water. Bring to the boil and pour away the water. Remove the skin from the almonds. Blend with soy milk until they are as fine as possible.

>> Bring the water to the boil with the agar agar powder and vanilla seeds and let it boil for 2-3 minutes.

>> Blend the agar agar mixture with the almond mixture.

>> Pour the mousse immediately into small individual serving bowls and place in the fridge. The mousse is ready approx. 30 minutes later.

Strawberry mousse

Mango mousse

Almond mousse

Mrs Diemer's legendary TIVOLI cake

This is named Tivoli cake because it is crisp and soft and tastes like the scent of the Tivoli gardens in Copenhagen – mouth watering – like the scent of sweet vanilla, strawberry and candy floss. Serve with whipped cream.

Serves 6-8

2 sheets filo pastry
450 g strawberries, or half
   strawberries and half
   raspberries
3 egg whites
150 g sugar
Seeds of ½ vanilla pod
2 tbsp icing sugar

Serve with

250 ml whipping cream for
   whipped cream

≫ If frozen, defrost the filo pastry according to the instructions on the packet.

≫ Put the berries in an ovenproof dish of approx. 26 cm diameter.

≫ Whisk the egg whites with the sugar and vanilla seeds until quite stiff. Put the egg mixture over the berries.

≫ Fold the filo pastry on top of the meringue: Fold it carefully without breaking it. One piece should cover one half of the meringue, the other the other half.

≫ Place the icing sugar in a sieve and sprinkle over the pastry.

≫ Bake the cake in the middle of the oven at 180C/gas 4 for 15-20 minutes. The filo pastry should be golden brown and the icing sugar caramelised on most of the pastry. If it is not caramelised you can turn the oven up a little and put the cake a little higher in the oven – but make sure it does not burn.

≫ Whisk the cream and serve with the warm cake.

ENTERTAINING

party food
guest dinners
buffets

PARTY BUFFETS

These are suggestions for parties at home and away. Larger buffets, smaller dinners and grill food, and tips and ideas for making delicious vegetarian party food suitable for vegetarians and meat eaters.

Spring

- Quails eggs and vegetables with dukkah page 14
- Bean ragout with lovage pesto page 143
- Spring rolls page 53
- Buckwheat noodles with crisp vegetables and sesame mayo page 72
- The season's crisp salad with dressing of your choice page 101
- Fruit crumble with rhubarb page 201

Summer

- Bombay Bloody Mary shot page 16
- Everyday pie page 38
- Vietnamese summer rolls page 66
- Multi bean salad, use peppers instead of tomato page 74
- Cauliflower dill cream page 92
- Strawberry mousse with almond milk page 202

Autumn

- Vegetables baked with mango-soy marinade page 20
- Mushroom-walnut pâté page 41
- Celeriac cream with fresh goat's cheese page 92
- Japanese inspired red cabbage salad page 84
- Bean soup with pasta page 168
- Chocolate truffles page 195

Winter

- Cones of seaweed with quinoa and avocado cream page 19
- Fennel-bean muffins page 47
- Grilled polenta with mushroom sauce page 48
- White cabbage salad with dried nuts – using red cabbage page 84
- Sunday curry winter version page 149 or dahl page 146
- Tropical fruit coconut ice cream page 196

! You can also use the recipes as an inspiration for your own buffets: Use the different sections in the book to combine first courses, firm and wrapped items, hot dishes or soups, salads with different consistency and something sweet to finish. Make sure there are not too many heavy dishes with carbohydrates, including beans.

A VEGETARIAN comes for dinner

If you want to serve meat and/or fish and a vegetarian is also coming for dinner, you can make a few dishes that everyone can eat and serve the meat or fish as accompaniment. Making the same dish for everyone saves time, and if you make a special dish for your vegetarian guest you risk that the other guests will suddenly have helped themselves to the vegetarian's food because it looks so delicious.

If you are making a vegetable pie for example, you can use it as accompaniment to the meat. Mushroom-walnut pâté page 41 is an excellent 'meat substitute'.

When planning the menu choose the recipe you like the most and which is also filling. Make plenty of it. Supplement with a small roast, a salmon fillet or similar.

These are suggestions for how you can follow the seasons and combine the book's recipes for a dinner party, which will fill a vegetarian and can be supplemented with meat or fish:

Spring
Miso soup with pearl barley page 162
Mung bean salad page 74
Smoked cheese salad page 83

Summer
Polenta page 48 with tomato sauce page 113
Cauliflower dill cream page 92
Summer salad with dressing page 101
Bread page 184

Autumn
Creamy turnip potatoes 134
Multi-bean salad page 77
Autumn salad with dressing page 101
Bread page 184

Winter
Root vegetable lasagne page 129
Hummus page 87
Green cabbage salad page 83
Bread page 184

A MEAT EATER comes for dinner

If you are vegetarian and have meat eaters for dinner serve your own favourite dishes for Mr. or Mrs. Meat – and see what happens. As far as we know, nobody has died from the sight of a vegetarian meal. These are suggestions for dinners that are combined in such a way that they are substantial and filling and most meat eaters will not miss the meat.

This is how you follow the seasons and combine the book's recipes to make a three course guest dinner:

Spring
First course: Tofu with topping page 23
Main course: Rice in a bowl with Thai salad page 118
Dessert Mango mousse page 202

Summer
First course: Potato pizza with truffle oil page 58
Main course: Spinach quenelles page 30 with spinach
   and multi-bean salad page 77
Dessert: Tivoli cake page 204

Autumn
First course: Borscht page 164
Main course: Mushroom-walnut pâté page 41,
   mixed green salad and bread 184
Dessert: Fruit crumble 201

Winter
First course: Indian pea soup page 173
Main course: Chickpea pancakes page 62 with potato-
   spinach masala page 133 and raita page 96
Dessert: Chocolate truffles page 195

Long live traditions

For a vegetarian the festivals may be a bit of a mouthful. What do you do with the traditional dishes when you cannot serve meat as you normally do? Luckily there are many green elements in the food we serve at the festivals. Often you only need to tweak the menu a little for it to still be 'tasting' of Christmas or Easter. For Christmas Eve you can replace the roast duck with the mushroom-walnut pâté page 41 served with the traditional red cabbage and sugar potatoes. If you want to celebrate it differently you could serve the Filo packets with winter filling page 54.

Vegetarian food on the BARBECUE

Grilled vegetables always taste wonderful, but remember to make plenty – not only for the vegetarians since everyone will want to taste them. They are not very filling and therefore it is a good idea to combine them with a substantial salad. They do take quite a long time to prepare, so we suggest you serve a first course or snack before the barbecue.

Vegetables and fruit suitable for the barbecue
- The following vegetables are grilled whole : Asparagus, corn on the cob, potatoes, small onions, tomatoes, Portobello mushrooms, new potatoes and spring onions.
- Or you can cut the vegetables into smaller pieces and put them on wooden skewers which have been soaked in water for 15 minutes.
- Aubergines and courgettes are cut into thick slices.
- Fennel, cabbage and peppers are cut into wedges.
- Brush the vegetables with a little oil before grilling and sprinkle with salt and pepper.
- Grill directly over the barbecue until golden and tender.
- Arrange the grilled vegetables in a dish and drizzle with the dressing.

The dressing: Make a dressing of your choice page 102 and drizzle it over the grilled vegetables. Or serve with the dukkah page 14, miso dip page 24 or Tahini dressing page 84.

Other suitable items: Polenta page 48, firm tofu, the marinated kind, if available or soy sausages.

Good substantial salads to go with the vegetables: See under substantial salads page 72 and the creamy salads page 87.

GREEN first aid manual

Meat is king in the West and vegetarians do suffer prejudice which manifests itself in different ways. This is a first aid manual for vegetarians and their nearest describing the most common situations – embarrassing, irritating, tiresome or just funny – and giving hints for what to do. The solution to the challenge depends very much on who is boss in the kitchen – battle axes have more power than you can imagine.

Help! I want to become vegetarian but the rest of the family don't want to.

It doesn't matter. You can easily add a piece of meat or fish to any vegetarian dish, so everyone will be happy. Prepare stews for example, so you add a bit of meat or fish to the part of the stew you are serving for the meat eaters.

Help! The rest of the family want to become vegetarian, but I don't want to.

If you are the family's main cook you will have to force yourself to like the idea, since you will be the one who prepares the vegetarian food for most of the time. Unless you grab the opportunity and make it a condition that the newly converted vegetarians give a helping hand in the kitchen with or without you. Start with the recipes in this book – and when you have mastered these, it is time to improvise on your own. Simply add the meat as accompaniment to the vegetarian dishes. This does mean, of course, that it will often be meat and fish which can be prepared and served separately from the rest – e.g. steaks, chops, burgers, chicken or fillet. When you feel like a stew with meat or fish you can easily use the same ingredients e.g. for the pasta meat sauce, lasagne or soup. When the basic sauce is in place, you will just have to use two saucepans or dishes and add the meat to one of them.

Help! Our canteen is a vegetarian's nightmare.

If you have a canteen at your work place where sausages are mixed in with the pasta sauce, bacon with the omelette and the salad buffet is boring or not yet invented, you may have to take your own food from home. If you are used to exciting and varied vegetarian food, two sandwiches for lunch is far too boring in the long run. Think of the leftovers from yesterday's dinner, a wholemeal bun with hummus and green salad etc. Some workplaces have fridges, where you could store your fresh vegetables, cooked pasta etc. so you can cut or slice a lunch for yourself that will make your colleagues green with envy. See the chapter with ideas for packed lunches, pages 174-181.

Help! I cannot afford to buy everything organic.

All is not lost. Better to be non-organic than not vegetarian at all. The advantages by omitting meat are still many steps ahead, even if you are not always choosing the organic variety.

Help! I cannot be bothered to explain that I am vegetarian.

A solution only used in an emergency is to adapt a sufficiently pained expression and declare that you are allergic to meat. Some people are allergic to milk, others to eggs. Why not meat? You will at least avoid the intrusive questions about why you are vegetarian and whether it also doesn't hurt a cucumber to be cut into slices.

Help! I have fallen in love with a vegetarian.

Congratulations! You can look forward to many years with a happy partner who will have relatively few sick days. Statistically vegetarians have fewer serious illnesses, are brighter and live longer compared to many others. Your vegetarian partner loves delicious food prepared with meatless love. Use this book for inspiration.

Help! I have fallen in love with a meat eater.

Congratulations! Difference furthers understanding, you will probably be fine. See useful hints under 'Help! I want to become vegetarian but the rest of the family don't want to. It doesn't matter. Besides, we have noticed that the rest of the household will follow when the family dinner is steered in a new direction.

Help! My dog does not want to become vegetarian.

Some vegetarians really do serve vegetarian food to their pets, although according to the manuals their pets are mainly meat eaters, e.g. dogs and cats. If Fido puts his nose up at your boiled carrots whisper in his ear that the world's oldest dog is 27 years old and vegan just like Mahatma Gandhi and his dog! If this does not work go back to the dog's next best friend: dog food.

VEGETARIAN FOOD AWAY FROM HOME

As a vegetarian you do not need to leave your dietary habits at home when you are out and about. These are a few green bits of advice to vegetarians who venture out into the city and the world:

On holiday: order vegetarian food when you book your ticket. Take a good guide book to enable you to understand the menus – many countries have culinary traditions which are vegetarian by nature and so you may find more vegetarian choices than you might at home. If you want to plan the holiday's vegetarian pit stops more precisely use the guide to 300 vegetarian restaurants in Europe: *Vegetarian Europe* by Alex Bourke.

You are invited to dinner at non vegetarians: Tell them politely that you eat neither fish, meat nor shellfish when you receive the invitation. Your hosts will then be able to make the necessary allowances when they plan the menu. You could also suggest an easy solution which would not need special purchases, such as making some extra vegetables and dishes from the *Best Salads* series. Or take a dish yourself from the chapter Firm page 26 as an accompaniment to the dishes served.

At a restaurant There is no long glorious tradition in the restaurant business for having vegetarian food on the menu, but some gourmet restaurants are beginning to introduce it. The best chance for vegetarian excellence, apart from certain top restaurants, is to choose ethnic restaurants with food from the Middle East, India and Asia. In most places the chef will make a vegetarian meal if you ask for it, and many dishes may be adapted to vegetarians if the chef omits the meat. Tell the restaurant when you book the table.
The best thing to do which will please any chef and most definitely make your vegetarian dish more exciting is to book a table in good time and at the same time tell them that you are vegetarian. Actual vegetarian restaurants also exist but they are few and far between, so you will have to look on the internet. On http://www.veggieplaces.co.uk/, http://www.happycow.net/europe/england/ you will find a list of vegetarian restaurants.

Wholemeal noodles

Buckwheat noodles

White miso

Wasabi

Rice paper

Red miso

Short grain brown rice

Quinoa

TOFU

Pearl spelt

Brown basmati rice

Brown jasmine rice

Tahini

Dark, toasted sesame oil

Agar agar

Nigella, seeds from the plant 'Love in the Mist'

Nori seaweed

Good vegetable stock powder

Pickled sushi ginger

Ginger pieces in syrup

Coriander seeds

Wakame seaweed

Tofu

Caraway seeds

Tandoori

Aram seaweed

Star anise

Garam masala

Cloves

Fennel seeds

Smoked paprika

Cardamom seeds

good INGREDIENTS

The following special ingredients are healthy and taste delicious in vegetarian cooking (see photo pages 214-215).

Whole spelt, wholemeal pasta, buckwheat noodles, brown basmati rice and jasmine rice, pearl spelt, pearl barley and short brown rice

Forget about quick carbohydrates in white pasta and refined rice and choose wholegrains and cereals with plenty of fibre. Apart from tasting delicious they provide a lot of fibre which is healthy for both stomach and intestines and prevents a lot of illnesses. The good food fibres also give you an increased sense of feeling full and you will have a healthy thirst making you drink more water. Available from supermarkets and health food shops

Quinoa

There is nothing negative to say about quinoa, the South American "Golden Grain". Quinoa is a gluten-free seed of the chenopodiaceae family of plants. It tastes wonderful, is easy to use and is super healthy. If quinoa is part of your basic diet, you do not need to eat meat, unless of course you like the taste of meat. Quinoa is full of proteins with the perfect amino acid combination. Use it hot instead of rice etc. and cold like bulgur in salads. Available from supermarkets and health food shops.

Rice paper

Dried rice paper pancakes made from rice flour, round or square, small or large. Soak three-four sheets at a time in a bowl with cold water for a couple of minutes until they are pliable. If they stay for too long in the water they become too soft and lose texture. Remove one sheet at a time from the water, fill the sheet with vegetables and roll it up. The rice paper can be eaten without further preparation, deliciously light and soft but can also be deep fried. Available from Chinese and Thai specialist food shops

Miso

Miso is a fermented soy bean product, a staple ingredient in Japanese cuisine. Some people may know it as part of the soup served in sushi restaurants but miso can be used for much more, see for example the recipes page 23 and 24.

It is very healthy, allegedly good for hangovers and is an excellent flavour enhancer. There are many different types of miso. The 'white' rice miso has the mildest flavour, the 'red' rice miso has a slightly stronger flavour. The dark types which are not included in the photo are barley miso and soy bean miso; these have a very strong flavour. In Japan miso is available in many more qualities than we find in this country.

The dark miso is generally available from health food shops and some supermarkets, both kinds are usually available from Asian grocers.

Good vegetable stock

Buy good quality vegetable stock without additives from health food shops or supermarkets. Vegetable stock is sold as a paste, powder, liquid or in cubes.

Wasabi

Wasabi is a Japanese horseradish which is light green and very strong. Available as paste in a tube and as a powder to be mixed with water to a suitable consistency. Used for sushi and as a flavour enhancer in many dishes. All wasabis have different strengths, so find the one you like. Available from well stocked supermarkets and Asian grocers.

Tofu

Tofu is a Japanese soy bean product eaten daily in Japanese homes. Tofu is very healthy and you will feel full in a comfortable and pleasant way. In the West tofu is mainly used in vegetarian cooking, when you will often be disappointed since it looks like feta but without much flavour. If we had more Japanese tofu qualities in this country, we would be able to discover its diversity. Use silken tofu if the dish should not be too firm and the slightly coarser tofu or smoked tofu, if you want a firmer consistency or prefer the smoky flavour. Available from well stocked supermarkets and Asian grocers.

Ginger
The types of ginger we have used in this book have different flavour and can be used in different ways. Fresh ginger is peeled and grated or chopped finely and used in Indian and Asian dishes. Sushi-ginger is strong and acidic and can be used as a flavour enhancer in Japanese inspired salads, dressings and dishes. In the pink variety colouring has been used. Ginger in syrup is strong and sweet and can be used chopped as a flavour enhancer in curries and for sweet dishes.

Tahini
A paste of sesame seeds and salt which is absolutely necessary as a flavour enhancer in hummus. The best ones are Arabic and available from well stocked grocers but there are varieties also available from health food shops and in well stocked supermarkets.

Sesame Oil
Toasted dark sesame oil is a fantastic Asian flavour enhancer which is used both in cold and hot dishes. You will need only a few teaspoons for 4 people.

Seaweed
Dried Japanese seaweed is available in many different qualities for example: Nori seaweed sheets, which are used for wrapping sushi rolls and as strips for garnishing; wakame seaweed, which is used in salads and soups, turns green when boiled, hijiki and arame seaweed which is used in salad. Seaweed is very healthy and rich in proteins, contains many minerals and vitamins and helps to lower cholesterol and blood pressure. It has the best flavour when marinated. Available from health food shops and Asian grocers.

Agar agar
If you want to make a vegetarian mousse or other dessert that needs thickening, you can use agar agar. Leaf gelatine is naturally to be avoided since it is mainly made from pigs' ears.

Agar agar is a product made from algae which is super easy to use. It sets much more quickly than gelatine and you will not have lumps as often happens when gelatine fails to set properly. It is also nice to know that you are not eating pigs' ears with your dessert whether you are vegetarian or not.

Agar agar is available from health food shops. Buy it as a powder.

Japanese soy sauce
Soy sauce is a world of its own. There are almost as many soy sauce types as there are wines in France. Each district has its own soy sauce and the quality varies enormously. The best known and most widely available brand of soy sauce is Kikkoman which is good for marinades and sauces as it has a very strong flavour. Yamasa is lighter, less salty and less caramelised. Tamari which we have used in this book is a strong type which can be replaced with the milder variety. Available from Asian supermarkets and health food shops.

Smoked cheese
Rygeost is a soft cow's milk cheese, with a texture like fresh goat's cheese, exclusively found in Denmark. Often made with low fat milk, it is smoked and has just a touch of caraway seeds. It will add a piquant smoked flavour to many dressings. Mix it with yogurt or crème fraîche. You can also use it as topping for salads cut into small cubes à la feta cheese.

Nigella, small black seeds from the plant 'Love in the mist'
Traditionally used to sprinkle on top of bread like poppy seeds. Good as a flavour enhancer in potato salads, root vegetable salads etc. Should always be toasted in a pan or baked to bring out the flavour. Available from Asian grocers.

Whole spices
We have used cardamom, star anise, coriander, cloves, fennel seeds and cumin seeds in many dishes in this book. The photo shows you what they look like. The flavour is intensified if the spices are toasted in a dry hot pan until fragrant. Grind lightly in a mortar or coffee grinder. Available from health food shops and Asian grocers.

Ground spices

Garam masala and tandoori are Indian spice mixes which we have used in several recipes in the book. Mixtures vary, find the one you prefer. Available from Asian grocers and well stocked supermarkets. Smoked paprika is strong, gives a delicious smoked flavour, and works as the vegetarian's bacon.

Fats and oils

There is much confusion about fats and we cannot give you a final answer to what is healthy and less healthy. Not even the experts can give a definite answer. Here are a few guide lines where we combine gastronomic considerations with maximum health considerations.

Use (virgin) olive oil for Southern European and Arab dishes and the yellow cold pressed rapeseed oil for other dishes. If you want a neutral tasting oil for e.g. Indian, Asian and South American dishes choose the clear rapeseed oil. We have used coconut oil in a dessert as replacement for butter to make the dish vegan. We rarely use butter and then only in small quantities, where flavour demands it.

Full time vegetarians/vegans and anyone who does not eat oily fish should make sure that they have enough of the essential fatty acid Omega3. This is found in linseeds, pumpkin seeds and rapeseed oil or as a food supplement in the form of oil.

Umami

Umami is called the 5th basic taste – after the well known: sweet, sour, salty and bitter. Umami is the Japanese name for 'delicate' or ' good tasting' and since there is not a suitable name in English it is simply called umami. Umami can be described as meaning the food has 'flavour'. If for example, you taste a vegetable soup after 5 minutes cooking, it will not have much flavour. When it has been cooking for ½-1 hour, it will suddenly have 'flavour', indeed quite a lot. This is the umami kicking in.

Umami is particularly present in protein rich foods such as meat, fish, eggs and dairy products but also in some vegetables and in many of the good flavour elements used in vegetarian cooking. If you are using ingredients with umami you will complete the flavour experience and also satisfy meat lovers.

This is where you find vegetarian umami:
- In fermented foods, such as soy sauce, Worcester sauce, wine, beer and miso.
- In matured foods such as blue cheese and parmesan.
- In vegetables, tomatoes, onions, mushrooms, asparagus especially when cooked.
- In seaweed, sun-dried tomatoes and vegetable stock in yeast and fried tofu.
- In cooked foods, e.g. boiled, fried and baked potatoes, boiled beans and lentils.

Nothing will improve people's health and increase the chances for the survival of the planet as much as the development towards a vegetarian life style.
Albert Einstein,, Physicist

Cook's knife

Vegetable knife

Hand blender

PHILIPS

600 Watt

Potato peeler

Food processor

Vegetable grater

The vegetarian's TOOLS

You only need a few tools. Make sure knives are sharp and invest in a decent quality chopping board which sits firmly on the work top. Replace potato peelers, vegetable knives and vegetable graters regularly. When the kitchen work begins to slow down and becomes cumbersome, it is often because the tools have become a little dull. Have your knives sharpened and buy new potato peelers, vegetable knives and vegetable graters and you will find the work becomes easy again.

Cook's knife

A good quality cook's knife is one of the most important and indispensable tools in a kitchen, especially when you are cutting a lot of vegetables. Invest in a good quality one even if it is expensive. A knife of good quality will last a lifetime. It is made of steel which keeps its sharpness for a long time. It lies easily in your hand and suits you. It does most of the work when you need to cut large and hard vegetables, e.g. squash, cabbage and celeriac. If you need to cut smaller items use the pointed end. The knife should be sharpened on a steel now and then and be properly sharpened once a year.

Vegetable knife

A small vegetable knife is also a useful tool. It should not be serrated and is used for peeling garlic, ginger and Jerusalem artichokes. Buy one of good quality like the cook's knife, sharpen it now and then on the steel and properly once a year. A cheaper variety may also work but should be thrown away when it has become dull. Otherwise it is no longer fun to cook.

Potato peeler

A potato peeler is indispensable for potatoes and all root vegetables. Available in many varieties and the best are the ones which grip properly, cutting decent long strips. Unfortunately most of them are poor quality – do not put up with it! Replace it until you find one you like and it will be a lot more fun. Throw it away when it becomes dull.

Vegetable grater

A good vegetable grater should be stable on the chopping board, and have a good handle on top so you can get a good grip when grating large portions. The best ones have a large grating surface both for fine grating and coarse grating. Vegetable graters have a limited lifespan, they lose their sharpness and should then be replaced; however, they are quite inexpensive. If you need to slice something very thinly, it is better to use a mandolin grater which is available in many different qualities.

Hand blender

A good hand blender can be used for lots of different jobs: Blending soups, hummus, pestos, ice cream etc. It is easier to use if the mixture is quite liquidy, like soups, but it also works surprisingly well with drier mixtures such as hummus.

Food processor

This is very useful if you need to grate or slice a large quantity of vegetables. If you do not have a hand blender or the hand blender does not have enough power, it is also useful for the items mentioned above. You can also blend pancake batter and small root vegetable pancakes in a food processor.

Chopping board

A large good quality wooden chopping board is also worth investing in. With a sufficiently big chopping board, there is plenty of room for all the vegetables so you can arrange them in small groups in the order in which they go into the pot. The chopping board should be washed thoroughly and properly dried between each use. If you look after it and oil it now and then with a little cooking oil, it will last for many years. A few small plastic chopping boards are also useful and they can go in the dish washer.

! A bread knife with grated edge only used for bread.

The best ever TIPS for vegetables

Vegetarian cooking inevitably contains many vegetables. It therefore pays to have a system for washing and rinsing and cutting all your vegetables:

- Start by bringing out all the vegetables you will need for the dish.

- Clean all the vegetables. Fill the sink, washing bowl or salad drier with cold water and rinse the vegetables so you don't need to rinse each vegetable individually and waste a lot of pure drinking water.

- When all the vegetables are clean, remove all waste and packing material and clean the work top.

- Now it is time to cut the vegetables and it is much more fun when they are all clean and ready for use.

- Cut the vegetables as you like them: coarse, rustic or small, fine and neat. The preparation time will depend on the size. Cut all the vegetables which should be cooked together in the same size so they are ready at the same time. If you feel like a change cut the vegetables differently every day.

- Make sure that the vegetables have been cut so they suit the cooking method you have planned. For stir frying they should be cut very thinly, so they won't need cooking for too long before they are ready. For oven baking they should have a certain size in order not to dry out before they are ready.

- Coarse vegetables to be eaten raw should not be cut into too large chunks, as it will take the pleasure away with too much chewing. Finely grated or coarsely grated so the dressing can adequately cover them, they are much easier to eat in 'raw' quantities.

- If there are several vegetables in a dish you can cut them small so you will have a bit of everything on the fork and have a complete taste experience. If you cut them coarsely you will have several different flavour experiences with each mouthful.

- Vary the cutting method: Long vegetables are beautiful when cut diagonally. Root vegetables can be cut into large, small or tiny cubes. Or into coarse or fine sticks, slices, triangles or other shapes, e.g. a carrot which is cut diagonally could be turned one third before cutting through it again etc.

- Vegetables for soups should always be cut so they can fit onto a spoon, otherwise it will be a splashy affair to eat.

- Conserve the beautiful form of the vegetables. Pointed cabbage, fennel, onions and chicory are very beautiful when cut into wedges and will keep their shape better than when cut into slices diagonally.

- Never boil vegetables in cold water, they lose flavour and vitamins and they may be ready long before the water gets to the boil. Use lightly salted boiling water and it is much easier to control the cooking time. Keep an eye on them to make sure they cook for long enough and do not overcook. A timer is very useful if you want to get on with other jobs in the meantime. Set the timer to a few minutes at a time.

- Serve the vegetables in soups and stews lightly crisp which gives the best flavour. If they are too raw they do not have much taste. If they are overcooked, the consistency and sometimes the flavour is not very exciting.

- Always use a small pointed knife to check the tenderness of vegetables – never a fork which leaves marks and gives resistance so the vegetables seem harder than they really are.

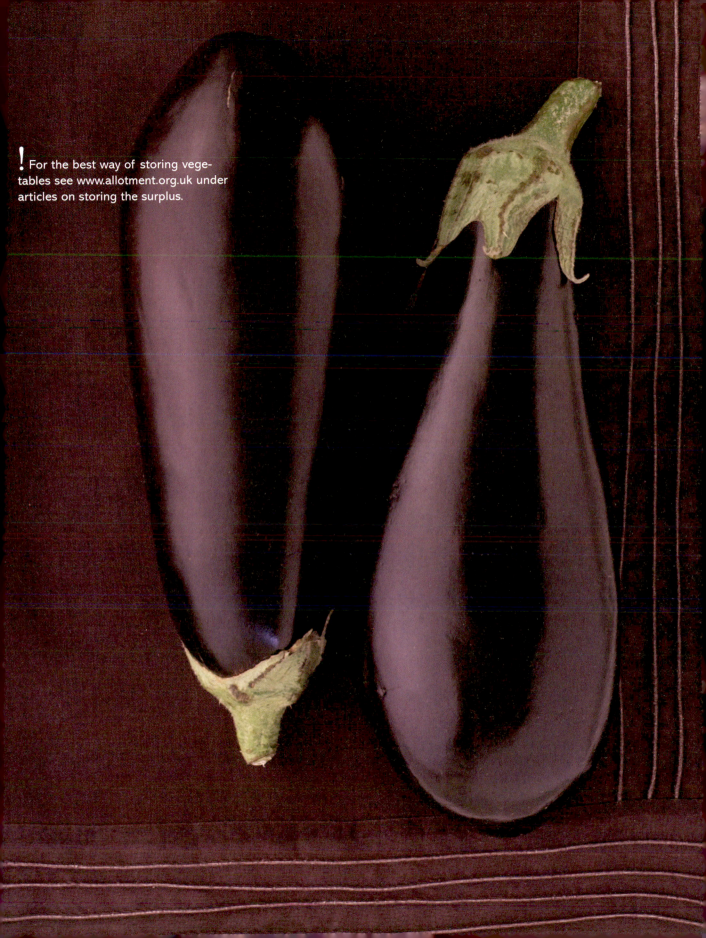

! For the best way of storing vegetables see www.allotment.org.uk under
articles on storing the surplus.

The best ever TIPS for beans

Beans are a wonderful source of protein for vegetarians and if you take our advice they will both taste delicious and be easier to deal with.

Break the bean barrier

One of the barriers to using beans is the necessary long term planning. You have to soak the beans the day before and cook them for up to several hours, though using a pressure cooker will greatly reduce the cooking time (see *The Basic Basics Pressure Cooker Cookbook* by Marguerite Patten). The following types do not need soaking: Mung beans, lentils, split peas and butter beans.

Great Bean day

You could also have a 'bean day' when you soak a large portion of several different kinds of beans the day before and boil them all at once the following day. Using different pots you keep an eye on them to make sure they are all cooked to perfection.

When they have cooled you put them into separate bags and freeze them. Freeze the beans in small bags or freeze them flat in larger bags, so you can break off the quantity you will need, this way you can have several different kinds of bean for dishes with a beautiful play of colour and form and shape.

Soaking and boiling

Soak the beans for at least 10-12 hours, or overnight in plenty of cold water. Discard the water. Always boil the beans in plenty of vegetable stock and use flavour enhancers such as dried or fresh herbs, onions, garlic and root vegetables. When boiling the beans use the same kind of vegetables and herbs that you will use in the recipe.

You cannot know beforehand precisely how long the beans will need. The same kinds of bean may have different cooking times depending on the label/harvest. They should be completely soft and tender. For many types of bean it may be 1½- 2 hours. Some beans, e.g. lentil and mung beans easily over cook – keep a sharp eye on these. Only add salt (remember vegetable stock may be salty) for the last few minutes of the cooking time, this will make them tender more quickly.

You can generally use the water from the beans but for some beans the water should be discarded due to the toxic properties which produce wind. For all the beans used in this book you can use the water they were boiled in.

"Caraway seeds with split peas reduce wind"

Boil the beans with caraway, cumin and fennel seeds – together or separately. If you want flavour from the spices use them for seasoning after cooking. This will give more flavour.

The best ever bean tips

A mistake made by many cooks is to not add enough vegetables to bean dishes, which makes the dish too heavy and rather boring. Dishes with beans taste best and will be much lighter if they contain vegetables and boiled beans in the ratio of 1:1 or preferably more vegetables than beans.

Flavour and succulence

For a suitable contrast mix the floury with crisp, raw vegetables and juicy boiled vegetables. Blending some of the beans or the lentils will also add a creamy texture to the dish. Season with something acidic, e.g. vinegar and lemon juice and something sharp, e.g. raw onions, mustard, horseradish, rocket or chilli.

Serve with

Boiled rice and whole quinoa is delicious with the bean dishes and the rice complements the beans with proteins.

SEASONAL chart for fruit and vegetables

 = season means that the produce is available.

= high season means that it is the optimum period for the fruit and vegetable and there is more of it.

Therefore we should use vegetables and fruit when in season:

- They taste better because they are super fresh and naturally ripened.
- They have not been transported from the other side of the world – damaging the environment.
- It will give you variety for your meals throughout the year so you don't end up eating tomatoes, cucumbers or broccoli every day.
- The variation will help you cover your nutritional requirements.
- It is often cheaper.

Use the seasonal chart when planning your menu

Make dishes from the ingredients which are in high season or season.

When you have found the vegetables and fruit which are in season in the chart, use the index on page 228 to find dishes with these ingredients.

Season for fruit, berries and nuts from open ground

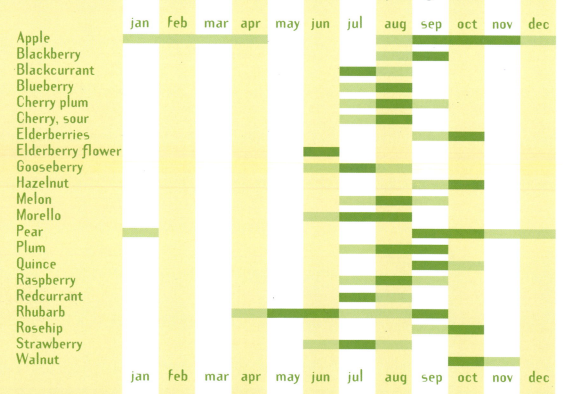

	jan	feb	mar	apr	may	jun	jul	aug	sep	oct	nov	dec
Apple												
Blackberry												
Blackcurrant												
Blueberry												
Cherry plum												
Cherry, sour												
Elderberries												
Elderberry flower												
Gooseberry												
Hazelnut												
Melon												
Morello												
Pear												
Plum												
Quince												
Raspberry												
Redcurrant												
Rhubarb												
Rosehip												
Strawberry												
Walnut												

Season for vegetables from open ground and under cover

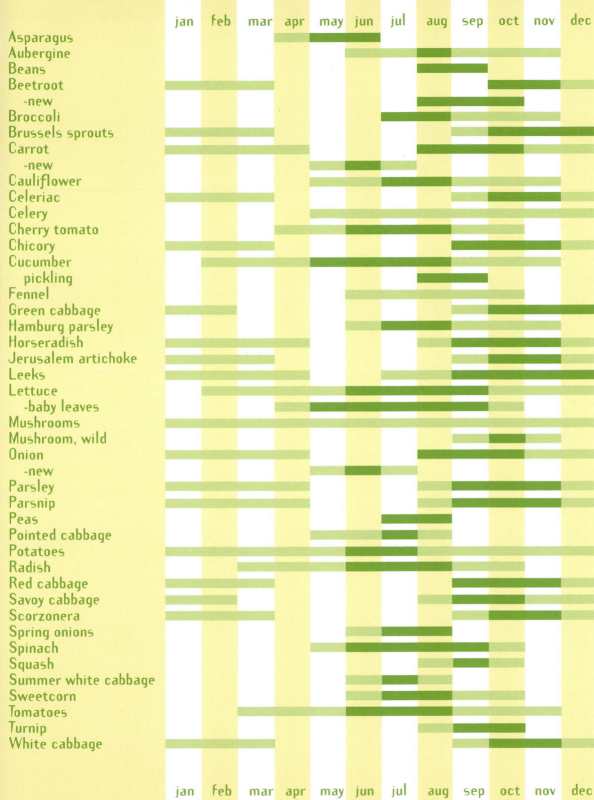

	jan	feb	mar	apr	may	jun	jul	aug	sep	oct	nov	dec
Asparagus												
Aubergine												
Beans												
Beetroot												
-new												
Broccoli												
Brussels sprouts												
Carrot												
-new												
Cauliflower												
Celeriac												
Celery												
Cherry tomato												
Chicory												
Cucumber												
pickling												
Fennel												
Green cabbage												
Hamburg parsley												
Horseradish												
Jerusalem artichoke												
Leeks												
Lettuce												
-baby leaves												
Mushrooms												
Mushroom, wild												
Onion												
-new												
Parsley												
Parsnip												
Peas												
Pointed cabbage												
Potatoes												
Radish												
Red cabbage												
Savoy cabbage												
Scorzonera												
Spring onions												
Spinach												
Squash												
Summer white cabbage												
Sweetcorn												
Tomatoes												
Turnip												
White cabbage												

jan	feb	mar	apr	may	jun	jul	aug	sep	oct	nov	dec

Seasonal Chart for Fruit and Vegetables

INDEX

The team behind the BOOK

Tina Scheftelowitz
Food writer, cookbook writer, product and concept developer, entrepreneur. Mother of Flora's Coffee bar and Amokka, developer of healthy fast food for supermarkets, consultant for cafees and restaurants, lecturer, runs courses, food writer for the Monthly magazine IN and Politiken. Writer of several cookbooks, see page 233. Through voluntary work supported the Danish Red Cross and The Danish Refugee Council, among others. Born 1964 and educated as a kitchen manager.
www.salathovederne.dk

Christine Bille Nielsen
Trained chef and nutrition- and domestic science economist. Previously chef at the Copenhagen Italian gourmet restaurant Era Ora. Food writer, food stylist, lecturer, teacher and product and concept developer for restaurants and food companies.

www.christinebillenielsen.dk
Fru Knips
Find the photographer at www.fruknips.dk.

Ruth Fabricius
Textile designer, illustrator and graphic designer, trained at Denmark's Design College and with Jesper Gundersen founder of the textile company Kurage. Works primarily with design of textiles, carpets and porcelain. Projects with decoration, logo design and packing for Flora's Coffee bar and Amokka A/S among others. Supported the Danish Refugee Council, The Danish Heart Association and Danish Red Cross as a volunteer. www.kurage.com

Lone Spliid
Free lance text writer and a wannnebe vegetarian. Training: Typewriting course (1975) supplemented with cand-phil in Literature. Book projects: *Boserups kærlighed, leg med din baby, ej sikke leg, skuespilhuset* etc. You will find the entire scrap book at www.spliid.com

All normal people love meat. You don't win friends with salad.
Homer Simpson

Thanks to the following:

Beautiful ceramics from Hanne Bertelsen www. hannebertelsen.dk. Porcelain Pillivuyt Babette from Thuesen Jensen tel. + 45 36 13 09 20 for nearest supplier and from Rikke Jakobsen www.rikkejakob-sen.com. Spoons from Stelton www.stelton.dk. Pots from Le Creuset Scandinavia.

Big thank you to

Ruth Fabricius who arranged the fantastic design of the book, to Henriette Wiberg Danielsen who has brought the design to the end. Mrs Knips who has taken the beautiful photos in the book. Annette Thanning and Lars Hansen-Damm who have created the book's title and subtitle. Lone Spli-id who has written the fine texts in the book, Ulla Mervild who has edited her way through all the vegetables. Janne Hedegaard Hansen who was a good sparring partner and tested the recipes. The participants in our trial dinner and focus group: Janne Hedegaard Hansen, Helena Heinesen Rebensdorff and Andreas Keith Hansen, Gitte Rosenfeldt Larsen, Helle Berkowith og Maria Wichmann Berkowitz. Dorte Ericsen and Kim Jensen and The Vegan Tasting Panel with Sofie Viborg Jensen, Nikolas Viborg and Amaya and their friends. Bille's brother Søren and the favourite sister in law Anita for vegetarian inspiration way back in our very early years. Bille's hard working work experience student Maj-Britt Andreasen, who went all the way to Lejre and helped us during the first confused photo days. Thank you for Marten Sørensen's scientific bean advice. Lisbet Diemer for wild gastronomic ideas who is always an inspiration and for making so many people happy with the recipe for the Tivoli cake page 232. Thank you to Sofiebader for loan of the beautiful bath tub for the vegevirgins on page 232 www.sofie-badet.dk. Alberte Meldahl Clemen with good input. Tina's family who have done without meat and fish for many days.

The publisher wishes to thank The Vegetarian Society of the United Kingdom and especially Su Taylor, the Press Officer and Gilly in the Research and Information Department for supplying all the up to date information about vegetarianism in the UK in pages 6-10. For general enquiries contact info@vegsoc.org or Tel: 0161 925 2000

This English language edition published in 2010 by Grub Street
4 Rainham Close
London
SW11 6SS
Email: food@grubstreet.co.uk
Web: www.grubstreet.co.uk

Copyright © Politikens Forlagshus A/S, 2008
Copyright this English language edition
© Grub Street 2010

Translation by Anne Marie Tremlett
Photos by Mrs Knips
English formatting and design: Sarah Driver

ISBN: 978-1-90650279-9
A catalogue record for this title is available from the British library

Printed and bound in Slovenia.